ON GASLIGHTING

INSIGHTS: PHILOSOPHY IN FOCUS

Elizabeth Harman, Series Editor

On Gaslighting

KATE ABRAMSON

PRINCETON UNIVERSITY PRESS

PRINCETON & OXFORD

Published by Princeton University Press
41 William Street, Princeton, New Jersey 08540
99 Banbury Road, Oxford OX2 6JX

press.princeton.edu

All Rights Reserved

ISBN 978-0-691-24938-4
ISBN (e-book) 978-0-691-24939-1

British Library Cataloging-in-Publication Data is available

Editorial: Matt Rohal and Alena Chekanov
Production Editorial: Jenny Wolkowicki
Jacket design: Karl Spurzem
Production: Erin Suydam
Publicity: Alyssa Sanford and Carmen Jimenez
Copyeditor: Joseph Dahm

This book has been composed in Arno Pro

Printed in the United States of America

10 9 8 7 6 5 4 3 2 1

Let me hold your crown, babe

—SARA BAREILLES

CONTENTS

ACKNOWLEDGMENTS

I STILL remember the sense of revelation I had when first introduced to the notion of gaslighting. I've now seen that look of stunned discovery on a great many faces. But as every philosopher worth their salt knows, traveling the path from any such initial feeling of insight to an account that is rich and rigorous enough to bear scrutiny is long, arduous, sometimes outright painful, and a journey that succeeds only if one has a lot of help. I have been extremely lucky in that last respect. My interlocutors have been both astute and generous with their time. This is my chance to express my gratitude, though my thanks will inevitably be inadequate.

I presented early versions of the chapters of this book in both colloquia and conference settings and gained a great deal from my interactions with the audience each time. My thanks in that light to all those who attended talks on these topics at Northwestern University, Vanderbilt, "Gaslighting and Epistemic Injustice" at Claremont McKenna (2017), and keynotes at the 2018 Annual Humphrey's Colloquium at the University of Louisville and the Minorities and Philosophy National Conference of 2021 at Florida State. A special thanks here goes out to the Minorities and Philosophy organizers at Yale University, who in 2013 invited me to give a talk, which turned out to be the earliest version of my first article on gaslighting. That article would, in turn, become the seed for this book.

I have benefitted enormously from conversations about each and all the arguments in this book. My gratitude goes out, in particular, to Julia Annas, Susanne Bobzien, Steve Darwall, Rachana Kamtekar, Jennifer Lackey, Lauren Leydon-Hardy, Cathay Liu, Kirk Ludwig, and Michelle Mason. I'd also like to extend my appreciation to two very thoughtful anonymous referees who helped me see what I did not see. For consistent support throughout the long process, I thank my sister Sarah, Mark Kaplan, David Sussman, Joan Weiner, and "the little engines." Some institutions have "in house counsel"; in the best possible sense, Gary Ebbs is my "in town analytic philosopher." I have benefitted incalculably from his precision and curiosity in working out the argumentative lines of this book. Adam Leite has been involved in this project from before its beginning, has read more drafts of chapters and bits of chapters than I care to count, and has spent long hours disagreeing and agreeing with me at each stage. This is a better book, and I'm a better philosopher, for it.

Last but hardly least, I cannot thank enough Elizabeth Harman, Matt Rohal, Rob Tempio, and Princeton University Press. Philosophers—get you an editor like Liz. Her ability to nudge a project toward its best overall shape, her enormous care and acuteness in reading through manuscript revisions—these she has at a level about which we mere authors fantasize. Matt Rohal has been enormously helpful, kind, and thorough at every stage and acted with the patience of a saint. Rob Tempio and the press understood from the beginning what I was trying to accomplish, and I deeply appreciate their encouragement at every stage.

Introduction to Our Topic

That's crazy.
  Don't be so sensitive.
That's all in <u>you</u>.
  It doesn't <u>mean</u> anything
That never happened.
  It didn't happen like that.
There's no pattern.
  Don't you dare suggest that!
You're so suspicious.
  You're imagining things.
Don't be paranoid.
  I was just joking!
I didn't say that!
  I didn't mean that!
You're overreacting.
  Don't get so worked up.
If you're going to be like this, I can't talk to you.
  It wouldn't be any different anywhere else.
You're just acting out.
  I'm worried; I think you're not well.[1]

---

1. A version of this list first appeared in my 2014 article. I make use of portions of this article throughout.

Things gaslighters say. More or less subtle, more or less direct, all recognizable even if only after the fact. The term "gaslighting" comes from the movie *Gaslight* (1944), in which Gregory tries to make his spouse Paula lose her mind by manipulating her, her friends, and her physical environment.[2] Gregory seeks to have Paula hospitalized for mental instability so he can gain access to her jewels. We witness him engaging in one "crazy-making," manipulative move after another, over a stretch of months. At one point, for instance, he takes a brooch he's claimed to be a prized heirloom out of Paula's purse to make her question her memory of having put it there and nurse the seeds of her self-doubt. He places his own watch in her purse when she's not looking, accuses her of stealing it, and then "discovers" it while she is in the company of friends whom—unbeknownst to Paula—he has warned that Paula is unstable. This last incident not only upsets Paula but is constructed by Gregory to be public and so provide her friends with apparent "evidence" that she is losing her mind. It also thereby contributes to Paula's increasing isolation. The title of the movie is drawn from the following manipulative move. Gregory regularly searches for Paula's jewels in the attic, and when he does so, his turning on the lights there has the effect of diming the gaslights elsewhere in the house. Every time this happens Paula asks him why the gaslights have dimmed. And every time Gregory denies that any such thing has happened, insists

2. There's a reason I refer to this character as Gregory rather than his true name, Sergis: to understand what happened to Paula, we have to imaginatively enter into the perspective from which she was vulnerable to his manipulations. From that perspective, he was Gregory, her beloved husband.

Paula is imagining things, and suggests that this too is a sign of her growing mental illness. All the while Gregory is full of expressions of purported concern, including "Why don't you rest a while?," "Do you really want to go out?," and "You know you haven't been well."

In the 1980s "gaslighting" became a term of art in therapeutic practice and thereafter gradually made its way into selective colloquial usage.[3] From 2012 to 2014, as I presented the material that would become my first article on the subject, only a small minority of academic audiences were already familiar with the term. That's not surprising—it was used only occasionally in the popular press, there was virtually no academic discussion of gaslighting, and the philosophical literature contained only a couple of glancing mentions of the concept. Still, every audience member immediately recognized the phenomenon when I described it.

Since then the term "gaslighting" has entered the colloquial lexicon. It appears regularly in the pages of the *New York Times* and the *Washington Post*, as a topic of discussion on CNN, on countless blogs, and across social media. There are so many memes about gaslighting that entire subgenres have developed. The Chicks (formerly Dixie Chicks) have an album titled *Gaslighter*. Its usage crosses virtually every political line. And there's been a commensurate surge in academic theorizing about gaslighting.

When a term gains popular traction on this scale, the scope of phenomena referred to under its rubric inevitably shifts.

3. Gaslighting was first mentioned in the psychological literature in Barton and Whitehead (1969) and first discussed in Calef and Weinshel (1981).

"Gaslighting," accordingly, refers sometimes to a quite wide array of ways in which one person might relate to another, while at other times to a fairly narrow band of interpersonal interactions. One might treat these differences as merely verbal disputes. But we shouldn't. For one, expanding the term to cover all the varied phenomena sometimes now referred to as "gaslighting" runs the real risk of what's come to be called "semantic bleaching" or "concept creep," where a once powerful concept becomes little more than a tag of disapproval attached to otherwise disparate phenomena. In philosophical terms, it's making a thin ethical concept out of what used to be a thick one.

But there's an even more important reason to resist dramatic expansion of the class of phenomena referred to as "gaslighting." There is a real, immediately recognizable interpersonal phenomenon picked out by the term "gaslighting," and if we expand the territory covered by the term too much, we will lose sight of and lose our ability to name *that* phenomenon. Gaslighting in this sense—the sense so aptly captured by the movie—is different from lying, dismissing or ignoring someone. It's very different from familiar forms of manipulation like guilt-tripping and from familiar ways of making someone feel badly about themselves like shaming. It's different from not treating them as a credible source of information, and different from not taking them seriously in some other way. It is even different from "brainwashing" someone in the manner of a cult leader manipulating his followers into believing some outrageous falsehood. No such description of other forms of familiar ways of acting badly aptly characterizes what Gregory was up to in his interactions with Paula. When we want a quick one-line summary, we say that Gregory was trying to drive Paula crazy. A substantial portion of this monograph is devoted to spelling out, in detail, exactly what we are trying to capture about the phenomenon when we say that.

Notably, this close examination is premised on the thought that gaslighting is best understood as a form of *interpersonal interaction* rather than as a feature of social structures. To put it a bit starkly, people gaslight, social structures don't. That doesn't mean that there are no important links between social structures and gaslighting. Certain pernicious social structures—such as those involved in systematic racism and sexism—can play specifiable and significant roles in gaslighting. In fact, once we see just what those roles are, we will also be able to understand why some have found it so tempting to (mistakenly) think that it's the social structures themselves that, as it were, "do the gaslighting."

A crucial reason to get as clear as we can about all of this is that in being a distinctive interpersonal phenomenon, gaslighting is also a distinctive *moral* phenomenon. In fact, as we'll see, these two dimensions of gaslighting are inextricably linked. We can to some extent mark out what distinguishes gaslighting as an interpersonal phenomenon without making any specifically moral claims. But insofar as we wish to distinguish gaslighting from other nearby experiences—like conning someone or infantilizing her—we will inevitably in part be making a moral case, arguing that there are moral reasons to distinguish gaslighting from these other morally problematic ways of interacting with someone. Moreover, because gaslighting is a distinctive moral phenomenon, if we want to understand gaslighting, we need to find as precise and illuminating ways as we can to talk about what's wrong—horribly wrong, immoral, unethical, vicious—in interacting with someone *this* way. We can thereby gain not only a more complete and appropriately complicated picture of gaslighting but also a better understanding of the relationship in which gaslighting stands to other nearby moral phenomenon, like treating someone dismissively, lying to her, and "brainwashing" her.

One final dimension of gaslighting—both as a distinctive interpersonal phenomenon and as a distinct moral phenomenon—deserves separate treatment, namely, the relationship between trust and gaslighting. Although matters of *trust* are frequently mentioned in discussions of gaslighting, there's a whole nexus of questions about trust and its relationship to gaslighting that the literature has not addressed. For instance, *of course* it's true that gaslighters exploit their targets' trust. But exploit in what way(s)? Is it just like (or mostly like) the way in which a successful liar exploits her target's trust? I argue that it is not. Is trust used against the targets of gaslighting in just the way that gaslighters make pernicious use of their target's empathetic abilities, or their own positions of authority, or some other common tool of gaslighters? I argue that it is not. Rather, gaslighters exploit their targets' trust in ways that specifically take aim at the normative structure of trust. Similarly, it's obvious that gaslighting violates the target's trust. I argue however that the way that trust is thereby violated is importantly different from the ways in which other aspects of the interpersonal relationship are violated in gaslighting. Moreover, by thinking closely and carefully about how exactly trust is manipulated and fractured in gaslighting, we can also deepen our understanding of trust and its structure.

The organization of the monograph largely follows the narrative just outlined. In chapter 1 I propose an initial characterization of gaslighting and defend its key elements against the outlines of some alternatives that have recently emerged. This is followed, in chapter 2, by a general analysis of some of the typical contexts in which gaslighting occurs along with a series of examples. The purpose of this chapter is to provide material from everyday life on the basis of which we can pursue the more refined analysis of the phenomenon of gaslighting that follows in subsequent chapters. Chapter 3 takes a close look at the characteristic aims of the gaslighter, and chapter 4 examines the paradigmatic methods, means, and tools of gaslighting. In chapter 5 I argue against the recent expansion of the concept to include what's now called "structural gaslighting." Instead, I argue, if we reserve the term "gaslighting" for the kind of interpersonal cases identified in chapters 1 to 4, the *analogies and disanalogies* between gaslighting and other politically significant phenomena become mutually illuminating. In chapter 6 I turn my attention directly to examining gaslighting as a moral phenomenon. The central aims of this chapter are to explicate each of the many dimensions of the immorality of gaslighting, argue that none is reducible to any of the others, and make a case thereby that part of what makes gaslighting so awful is the multidimensional nature of its immorality. Finally, in chapter 7 I examine the various roles that trust plays in gaslighting. I argue that we can be much more specific than any existing account has been about the ways in which gaslighters use trust as a weapon, violate their target's trust, and damage their target's ability to trust. This will also allow us to bring into view significant features of interpersonal trust that have been overlooked in the philosophical literature.

My central goal is to offer an account of gaslighting that fits with, and allows us to make sense of, the phenomenon as we find it in everyday life. Doing so can illuminate a dark corner—both in the sense of not otherwise seen and in the sense of morally dark—of everyday life.

1

What Is Gaslighting?

A FIRST PASS

PART OF WHAT makes the great films from the forties and fifties so brilliant is the way they manage to capture messy truths about the human condition through a particular kind of stylized caricature. Such is certainly the case with *Gaslight*—that's the reason its portrayal of the sinister Gregory's interactions with his spouse Paula is the source of our twenty-first-century term.

But Gregory is, after all, a caricature. For the most part, even those whose character and conduct come closest to the fictional Gregory's differ from him in three respects. First, those who engage in this form of emotional manipulation are often not *consciously* trying to drive their targets crazy. Second, they often seem not to have any clear (further) end in view; they're not, that is, trying to drive their targets crazy for the sake of something so simply and straightforwardly understood as expensive jewels. Third, while Gregory was quite literally trying to drive Paula crazy—he wanted to maneuver her into a condition

9

where it would be appropriate to have her committed to a mental institution—gaslighters aren't typically trying to drive their targets crazy in quite that literal sense.

And yet gaslighting in the movie and in everyday life is nevertheless recognizably the same phenomenon. Very roughly, the core phenomenon that's come to be picked out with that term is a form of emotional manipulation in which the gaslighter tries (consciously or not) to induce in another not only the sense that her reactions, perceptions, memories, and/or beliefs are so utterly without grounds as to qualify as "crazy," but also the sense that she isn't capable of forming apt beliefs, perceptions, reactions, and so on. Furthermore, the gaslighter aims make it the case that the target's sense of herself in these respects is, in some sense, tracking a reality. In aphoristic form, the gaslighter is both trying to make the target think that she's crazy and trying to actually drive her crazy.

My use of the word "crazy" in this context is a deliberate choice that follows much of common usage and many dictionary definitions. These everyday definitions characterize gaslighting someone as "manipulat[ing] by psychological means into questioning his or her own sanity," a process that leaves a person "confused, anxious unable to trust themselves," and as a process is meant to "drive [someone] crazy."[1] Such uses of the word "crazy" and its synonyms in common definitions of gaslighting are, in my view, colloquial shorthands for features that are core to the phenomenon of gaslighting itself. First, there's the fact that "crazy" is a pejorative, and

---

1. *Oxford English Dictionary*, 2022; Duignan, 2017; Hammond, 2017.

a pejorative of a particular kind.[2] Gaslighting, when successful, results in the target's feeling badly about herself, but not just badly in any old way: it's not mere guilt-tripping or shaming (as awful as those can be). Dictionary and colloquial definitions try to capture the very particular way in which someone who has been gaslit is induced to feel badly about herself by speaking in terms of the target's "feeling crazy" or "questioning her sanity." Second, everyday descriptions of gaslighting as a process meant to "drive someone crazy" are efforts to capture through common colloquialism the fact that the gaslighter is trying to *do something to* the psychology of his target, something that will fundamentally undermine her. These core features of gaslighting demand close consideration, even as we proceed knowing that the word "crazy" can mislead in quite problematic ways if we're not very careful.

I've already suggested that we shouldn't take "crazy" literally here. Successful gaslighting does have serious clinical consequences—paradigmatically, depression. But it is not clinical depression at which gaslighters aim, nor is that what lies behind the common thought that gaslighters are trying to drive their targets crazy. And yet that thought is not mere hyperbole. It's not even quite metaphor. It's a colloquialism, a shorthand that's trying to point to the ways in which gaslighting is aimed

2. Some writers have urged that precisely because "crazy" is pejorative, and for that reason offensive to those who have psychiatric conditions and/or mental illnesses, we should avoid all use of the term. For reasons noted above, I disagree: in this case, the pejorative conations of "crazy" are part of the point—the gaslighter wants his target to feel badly about herself in *the way that term communicates*. This aspect of the gaslighter's motives is explored in more detail in both chapter 3 (on the aims of gaslighting) and chapter 6 (on its immorality).

at radically undermining a person's *ability* to engage with the world reasonably, appropriately, and in psychologically healthy ways. Further specification and elucidation of this dimension of gaslighting will take the work of the next three chapters. For now, what's important is that the everyday notions of gaslighting (rightly in my view) pick up on the thought that, like Gregory, gaslighters aren't just trying to make their targets *think* that they are unwell or incapacitated: they are trying to incapacitate them.

1. The Question at Hand

Gaslighting thus described is quite unlike other ways of ill-treating someone—say, dismissing them. To dismiss someone is to fail to take her seriously. The gaslighter is trying to get his target not to take *herself* seriously. And he's trying to create conditions such that it will be *appropriate* for neither her nor anyone else to take her seriously. There are other contrasts with ordinary dismissiveness as well. Gaslighting, for instance, involves multiple incidents that take place over long stretches of time; it frequently involves multiple parties playing the role of gaslighter or cooperating with a gaslighter; it frequently involves isolating the target. And then there are the characteristic things gaslighters say: indeed, for all the ways in which Gregory is a stylized caricature of his real-life counterparts, it is remarkable how much overlap there is between the phrases that Gregory uses to undermine Paula in the movie and those employed by gaslighters against their targets in real life. You recognized the phrases with which I opened this book, didn't you? There's a reason for that.

Still, there are other ways of characterizing gaslighting, in both popular and academic discussions. Some such alternatives treat gaslighting as a species of dismissal, or to read or contend that gaslighting needn't be intentional, or treat "gaslighting" as interchangeable with "conning," or describe any behavior that leaves the target feeling badly about herself without adequate warrant as gaslighting (such that ordinary "guilt-tripping" or shaming would qualify as gaslighting).

How are we to adjudicate among such very different ways of characterizing gaslighting? After all, we could resolve to use the term to pick out whatever phenomena we like. In what remains of this chapter I argue that my initial rough sketch of gaslighting has certain key features that any adequate conception of gaslighting must have. In that sense, this initial characterization of gaslighting will later provide something like the bones of an account that is to be refined and fleshed out in subsequent chapters. But the work of subsequent chapters also contributes to the overall argument in another way. I'm offering a critical interpretation and analysis of a complicated interpersonal phenomenon, and in that light there's an important respect in which the analysis of subsequent chapters offers not only arguments for further specifications of the account of gaslighting but also additional evidence that the initial characterization is apt. The case, in other words, is cumulative.

2. Gaslighting Basics

Here then, once again, is my proposed initial characterization of gaslighting:

> Gaslighting is a form of emotional manipulation in which the gaslighter tries (consciously or not) to induce in another not only the sense that her reactions, perceptions,

memories, and/or beliefs are so utterly without grounds as to qualify as "crazy," but also the sense that she isn't capable of forming apt beliefs, perceptions, reactions, and so on. Furthermore, the gaslighter aims to make it the case that the target's sense of herself in these respects is, in some sense, tracking a reality. In colloquial terms, the gaslighter is both trying to make her target think that she's crazy and trying to actually drive her crazy.

To see why any adequate account of gaslighting ought to include all of the basic elements we find in this initial sketch, let's begin in the least controversial place. Nearly all definitions of gaslighting include the thought that successful gaslighting will leave its target deeply doubting her own perceptions, reactions, judgments, and so on. This matters more than it might at first seem. Notice, for instance, that this state is different from that of changing one's beliefs, deciding that one's perceptions were wrong, or seeing things differently. It's different even from doing any of those things as a result of someone else's nefarious conduct (say, as a result of them lying or manipulating you). It is important to pay attention to this difference when we're thinking about how to characterize gaslighting for three reasons. First, while gaslighters are often not able to tolerate disagreement (we'll come back to that shortly), agreement isn't the endpoint of successful gaslighting. Second, this basic feature of gaslighting helps explain why *this* term arose in spite of the fact that we already had in common usage the term "brainwashing." The difference even shows up in dictionary definitions of the two. The *OED*, for instance, gives us "make (someone) adopt radically different beliefs by using systematic and often forcible pressure" as a definition of "brainwash" and "manipulate (someone) by psychological means into questioning their own sanity" as a definition of "gaslight." The experiences named by the terms "brainwashing" and "gaslighting" differ even at this level.

Here's a third, more subtle, reason to keep clear on this difference: once we see that changing (even radically) one's beliefs, perceptions, reactions, and so on is different from having the sense that one's beliefs, perceptions, reactions, and so on are so unfounded as to make one question one's sanity, we can also see that the latter doesn't even require the former. In fact, if one could change one's beliefs, perceptions, and so on, that might well be a way to avoid feeling insane. The target of gaslighting is stuck feeling insane in part because she *can't* make herself see things as her gaslighter claims they are. There's a scene in the movie *Gaslight*, for instance, where Gregory has taken a painting down from the wall, hidden it, and now insists to Paula that she must have removed it herself. At first, Paula is both adamant that she didn't do so and completely rattled by the accusation. After humiliating her in front of the servants whom he makes a show of querying about the painting, Gregory sends Paula upstairs to look for the painting. When she finds it he reiterates that she must have put it there. Again, she insists otherwise, saying that she only looked where it had been twice before. He retorts that she should go to her room, for she's clearly too unwell to go to the theater as planned. She folds, and collapses weeping, now genuinely unsure whether she's losing her mind. But she's still not convinced she moved the "little picture." This, the experience of being gaslit, is different from the experience of being "brainwashed" into believing something radically different from what one would otherwise believe.

My own initial characterization of gaslighting does go beyond some others in certain respects. To begin with, I've claimed that successful gaslighting will involve the target not only questioning her own sanity but also actually *being* incapacitated in some way plausibly captured by the colloquialism of "having been driven crazy." One might try to prize these two apart by thinking of the person who has been successfully gaslit as someone who doubts her sanity but whose deliberative, emotional, perceptual, and evaluative skills are in fact all fully intact. Crudely stated, on this view the person who has been successfully gaslit sees herself as insane, but she isn't. I think that's an untenable view about gaslighting for reasons that will fully emerge only in chapters 3 and 4—reasons having to do, on the one hand, with the nature of the (typical) gaslighter's motivational psychology and, on the other hand, with the difficulty of trying to maintain one's sanity (in the relevant sense) while radically doubting one's sanity in the sense relevant to gaslighting. For the time being, however, let me offer just a few general reasons not to think of the outcome of successful gaslighting as *only* "doubting one's own sanity" but not actually having one's sanity undermined. First, there's just the simple point that our canonical gaslighter—Gregory—in fact intended on actually driving his spouse insane. The whole game was to do so in order to get her hospitalized for mental instability. That's not a sideshow in what makes him recognizable (albeit as a caricature) in the way that the fact that he's after Paula's jewels is a sideshow. But second, and to foreshadow themes the details of which will emerge in later chapters, think about what it's like, or would be like, to come to have the sense that some wide swath of one's beliefs, perceptions, and reactions are so radically ungrounded as to count as crazy, and furthermore, to see oneself as unable to reliably form apt beliefs, perceptions, reactions and so on. Part of what it *is* to be psychologically well is to have at least a baseline or minimal confidence in one's beliefs, perceptions, general deliberative abilities, and reactions—such that, for instance, one will treat one's beliefs as prima facie good starting points in deliberation, and have enough basic confidence to undertake deliberation where one is uncertain. Someone who is seriously questioning her sanity in the ways that are relevant here lacks precisely that kind of baseline confidence. In this sense, it's close to definitional that someone who questions her sanity in the very particular way that's relevant in gaslighting is someone who is not psychologically well—not fully sane.

Being induced to doubt one's sanity in *this* sense, much less being driven (more) insane (than that), is not something that can happen as a result of a single interaction. Perhaps certain drugs could induce something like the relevant state of mind, but even if someone gave another person a drug with the intention of making them feel insane, we wouldn't be tempted to say that the latter had been gaslit. Gaslighting is something a person does (or some people do), through interpersonal interactions. And if "having been gaslit" is paradigmatically marked by the target's radically questioning her own sanity (her ability to engage with the world appropriately, on a variety of fronts), that's something that has to occur over time. This is another respect in which the movie is brilliant: as fragile as Paula is portrayed as being from the start, it still takes Gregory a long stretch of time, a variety of manipulative behaviors, and consistent malfeasance to get her to the point of doubting her own sanity. In this way, preserving an intelligible link between our conception of the activity of gaslighting and that which we understand as the paradigmatic condition of the person who "has been gaslit" requires that we conceive of the activity as something that takes place over an extended period.

This thought both fits with and is confirmed by the fact that if we really think of the kind of interaction that would—*were* it part of a pattern—be a moment of gaslighting behavior as instead entirely isolated and not part of any such pattern, then we lose our sense that what's at issue is gaslighting. Someone might doubt my perception of a particular event without adequate reason, or accuse me of overreacting in a particular case where that's an inapt accusation, without their doing so being remotely recognizable gaslighting. Suppose, for instance, that after the fiftieth time someone carelessly steps on my foot, I finally snap and yell, "What's wrong with you?!? Get off my foot!" You witness only that fiftieth foot-stepping and accuse me of overreacting. You'd be wrong to think mine an overreaction, but we wouldn't think you were "gaslighting" me. We'd just correct what we take to be your lack of relevant background information— "It's the fiftieth time they've stepped on her foot."

So, what do we need to say about the gaslighters themselves in order to get the phenomenon properly into view? There's been some suggestion in recent literature that the gaslighters might do what they do "unintentionally."[3] That suggestion simply

---

3. See, e.g., Shabot, 2019; McKinnon, 2017. For popular press counterparts, see, e.g., Simon, 2015; Griffith, 2021.

cannot be read to flatfootedly mean what it says. If the gas-lighters are acting, they are by definition doing *something* intentionally. The question is *what* they are doing intentionally, and what the relationship is between, on the one hand, their doing those sorts of intentional things and the reasons we say that what they're doing intentionally qualifies as gaslighting. Some of those who claim that gaslighting can be "uninten-tional" portray the core behavior involved in gaslighting as that of unduly doubting another's testimony. Sometimes this is further specified as unduly doubting another's testimony when that other person is a member of a socially stigmatized group and/or with regard to some harm the target has suf-fered. I take it, then, that the fundamental suggestion behind the claim that this can be "unintentional" is that the gaslighter need not intend that their target end up in the state we recognize as "having been gaslit"—radically doubting her own perceptions, judgments, deliberative abilities, and reactions and having those abilities of hers themselves seriously undermined—but can end up in such a state simply as a result of having her tes-timony unduly questioned, without anyone intending she end up in such a state.

But here again, if we follow the suggestion, we'll end up with a conception of gaslighting that's problematic along several di-mensions. First, this suggestion would muddle the connection between gaslighting behavior and the states that we treat as paradigmatic of having been gaslit. If a gaslighter aims to get his target to question her sanity and to undermine her sanity, then there is a straightforward and intimate connection between gaslighting behavior (behavior that, among other things, is guided by those aims) and the states we treat as paradigmatic of "having been gaslit"—those are precisely the states of mind at which the gaslighter aims. If, in contrast, gaslighting behavior is just any behavior in which the gaslighter unduly doubts the testimony of their target, the connection between that behavior and seriously questioning one's own sanity (much less having one's sanity undermined) is *at best* one of typical effects. And it's doubtful that we can even get that "typical effects" claim generated plausibly without adding further claims about the gaslighter's motivational psychology, her relationship to her target, and so on. There are, for instance, all sorts of internet folks who unduly doubt all testimony by women philosophers about sexism in the field. I have never been moved to doubt my own sanity (or experiences) as a result— I've been moved to feel irritated, and to ignore them. Are these typical reactions? I don't know. But it's not obvious that mine are atypical reactions, and to the extent that's true, it's really unclear what we are supposed to think *is* the connection, on the proposed view, between unduly doubting someone's testimony (which we are told defines gaslighting) and the state of questioning one's own sanity that's paradigmatic of having been gaslit. In fact, there doesn't even seem to be a single unified phenomenon at issue here.

Here's another, even more serious, worry about characterizing gaslighting behavior simply in terms of one person unduly doubting another's testimony, perception, or reaction: we already have serviceable everyday names, concepts, and categories for that kind of bad behavior. In everyday life, we say that these are ways of being dismissive or not taking someone seriously. And in philosophy, when such unwarranted doubts are held on account of prejudice against the person whose testimony, perception, or reaction is at issue, we have the technical category of "testimonial injustice."[4] Moreover, as we've already noted, not taking someone seriously and trying to get her not to take herself seriously are two very different interpersonal phenomena and the proposed conception of gaslighting behavior elides that difference. This is especially troubling given that there is a recognizable interpersonal phenomenon that involves the latter and for which the term "gaslighting" was invented because we otherwise lacked a way of naming that phenomenon.

For these reasons, among others, I think that if we want an adequate characterization of gaslighting, there's no avoiding talking about the gaslighter's motivational psychology. One possibility on this score that's gained some traction is the thought that what's key to the gaslighter's psychology as such is that they cannot tolerate disagreement. A psychoanalyst who wrote one of the earlier explorations of gaslighting as she saw it emerging in her clinical practice put it this way: "A gaslighter . . . can't tolerate the slightest challenge to the way he sees things. However he decides to explain the world to himself, that's how you must see it, too—or leave him prey to unbearable anxiety."[5] I do think, as we'll see in chapter 3, that something like this kind of deep anxiety often plays a significant role in the gaslighter's psychology. But I've come to think both that the motivational psychology of the gaslighter need not involve this anxious inability to tolerate disagreement, and that the inability to tolerate disagreement is insufficient to make someone a gaslighter. It's not necessary because, among other things, it turns

4. Fricker, 2007, 27.
5. Stern, 2007, Kindle location 275.

out that there are gaslighters in real life who are just as aware of their own motives as is Gregory—the whole package minus the search for the hidden jewels.[6] In cases like these, there's no need to posit unbearable anxiety about disagreement—these abusers are consciously aiming to drive their targets (usually spouses) mad. It's not sufficient to account for the psychology of gaslighters because someone who is unable to tolerate disagreement might be motivated by that disposition to act in many different ways, and some of them won't look at all like gaslighting. They might, for instance, just ignore or dismiss the dissenting voice, without showing any interest in inducing the dissenter to doubt her views, much less her own sanity. In fact, if your central motivating psychological state is the inability to tolerate disagreement, it seems it would be a lot easier to decide the dissenters don't count (and so can be ignored or dismissed) than to manipulate the dissenters into doubting their sanity.

The straightforward thing to say here is, as I've been urging, that the gaslighter aims to induce the states we already recognize as the hallmark of having been gaslit: in some sense, they are trying to make their target question her own sanity, while simultaneously also undermining her sanity. A full defense of this claim awaits in chapter 3, where I'll focus in more narrowly on the gaslighter's aims, try to diffuse any lingering doubts on this score, and spell out with more precision the senses in which someone who is gaslit both doubts her sanity and has it undermined. For now, however, we can see both that we cannot adequately characterize gaslighting without talking about the gaslighter's motivational psychology and that there isn't

6. See, e.g., Bowles, 2018; Zeiderman, 2019.

any obvious and plausible alternative to thinking about the gaslighter's motivational psychology in terms of such aims.

Now, I also claimed in my initial characterization of gaslighting that we needn't suppose that these aims are conscious. And yet given that I have already argued against other ways broadening the scope of what qualifies as gaslighting, one might wonder why I think this particular extension is a good one. After all, Gregory was conscious of what he was doing, and I've noted that, in that respect, he has real-life counterparts. The short answer to this question is that there's no good reason not to include unconscious (or, at any rate, not fully conscious) aims of the relevant sort. We recognize such aims routinely in everyday life—every time you accuse someone of acting passive-aggressively, "acting out," or "deflecting" (all words that originated in psychoanalytic contexts but that now have colloquial counterparts) you are attributing to them a nonconscious aim. Sometimes we blame people for such aims, sometimes we don't. But unconscious aims are no different in that respect from conscious aims. In this sense, there's also no obvious moral difference that would justify excluding behavior from the category of gaslighting on the grounds that the wrongdoer's aims were not conscious.

Finally, a few words concerning the last key part of my characterization of gaslighting about which I've yet to say anything: the claim that gaslighting takes place through manipulation. In one essential respect, the point of calling this a form of *manipulation* is extraordinarily simple: it's to mark into what general category of morally problematic interactions gaslighting belongs. For this purpose, it's important to stay close to everyday usage. In everyday usage, "manipulation" is a term of condemnation referring roughly to morally problematic ways of influencing or controlling others that are not reducible to force or forced choice.[7] Here the principal contrast categories are force/forced choice (e.g., threats), morally permissible or salutary ways of interacting with someone—e.g., reasoning with them, asking something of them, and other permissible or salutary ways of influencing others. Of course, in situ, some of what the gaslighter does can *look* like a permissible or salutary way of interacting with someone. "Have some empathy for the guy" can be, after all, an appropriate appeal. Or it can be manipulative in the ordinary sense of appealing to someone's emotions to get them to do what they do not on consideration judge to be the right thing to do. Or it can be part of a gaslighting pattern. The devil is in the details, as they say.

We have, in sum, good reasons to favor my initial characterization of gaslighting as a form of emotional manipulation in which the gaslighter tries (consciously or not) both to induce in someone the sense that her reactions, perceptions, memories, and/or beliefs are so utterly without grounds as to qualify as crazy and, furthermore, to make it the case that this sense of herself is, in some sense, in fact apt by radically undermining the abilities constitutive of being psychologically well. But to understand gaslighting as an interpersonal and moral phenomenon, we need to get much more specific than this. Our working characterization needs refinement. And to do that, we need to first know more about the phenomenon of which we speak. It is to that task we turn in chapter 2.

7. There are philosophers who propose technical conceptions of manipulation on which it is not necessarily morally problematic. E.g., Buss, 2005.

2

What Gaslighting Looks Like

THE KEYSTONE of this book is an interpretation and analysis of the interpersonal and moral dimensions of a form of interaction that occurs in everyday life: gaslighting. To accomplish this goal in any greater detail than that provided in chapter 1, we need to know more about what the interactions that are the basis for this interpretation and analysis look like. We need, in other words, examples. A bunch of them.

And yet gaslighting presents a number of difficulties on this score, difficulties to which we need to pay attention both in the choice of examples and in our interpretation of those examples. First, because gaslighters are often not consciously aware of their own aims, we shouldn't expect examples that involve explicitly articulated gaslighting aims. Second, as we've seen, gaslighting necessarily takes place over time, and that's difficult to capture in an example that describes a single episode. Indeed, no description of a single incident can quite capture the sense of iteration, the constant echoing drumbeat that it takes to become radically undermined via interpersonal interactions. Moreover, even if some particular incident involves someone conducting themselves in one of the ways that gas-lighters do, that incident may not form part of any pattern. People can say things like "that's crazy" in a one-off manner. And even where there is a pattern of conduct that consists in some of the things that gaslighters do—like lying—the pattern isn't always one of gaslighting. Lying, for instance, is a common tactic of both gaslighters and mere liars, but the behavior over time of mere liars involves a different pattern of behavior. So we have this basic problem: we need fairly detailed descriptions of particular incidents in order to get a fine-grained sense of what gaslighting is like in situ, but it's the larger context and pattern of interactions that would make those particular incidents qualify as gaslighting, and that larger context must be imagined or, at best, gestured toward.

For these reasons, in what follows I approach the need for examples in two ways. When gaslighting occurs, it often takes place in particular kinds of contexts. So to set a little bit of framework for interpreting particular examples, in what follows, I first describe in general terms some of the common contexts of gaslighting interactions. I then offer a series of examples that fit the initial characterization of gaslighting for which I argued in chapter 1 and involve one or more of those common contexts of gaslighting.

1. Common Gaslighting Contexts

A. Intimate Relationships

It's not a coincidence that the play and movie that gave rise to this term involve interactions between spouses. The early articles on the subject by psychologists and psychoanalysts were similarly concerned with gaslighting between spouses as well as the terrifying possibility of analysts gaslighting their analysands.[1] It's depressingly common among abusive parents as well—both as a form of abuse and as a way of covering up other forms of abuse (by gaslighting those who protest against it).[2]

In close adult relationships one is especially vulnerable to emotional manipulation. And there are reasons to think that those who engage in gaslighting may be more likely to do so in intimate contexts, not only because they *can* more readily do so but because it's more emotionally threatening for them to be challenged by an intimate. Most of us are more emotionally responsive to disagreements with loved ones than to disagreements with strangers. We react by feeling especially curious, or sad, or perhaps anxious about negotiating potential practical conflicts or conflicts in values. The gaslighter reacts by trying to make the challenge go away by configuring its source as crazy.

The abusive parent who gaslights is especially awful. Children are only just learning to manage their emotions, deliberations, and judgments. The people who are supposed to be teaching them this are those in parental roles. I'm not, however, going to discuss the gaslighting of children. There are too many special questions that arise in those cases that would require a different kind of work. Among other things, thinking about the gaslighting of children would require staking out views about child development because what we think of gaslighting as *doing to* a child will depend on our conception of child development.

1. Barton and Whitehead, 1969; Calef and Weinshel, 1981; Dorpat, 1996.
2. See, e.g., Kelsey-Sugg and Nur, 2019.

B. Protests Against Patterns of Bad Conduct

There are a wide variety of contexts in which gaslighting is deployed as a response to the target's protests against someone's bad conduct. Protests against bad conduct in the workplace are one subspecies.[3] So too is the kind of "mean girl" behavior meant not just to make someone miserable but to lose their grip on reality.[4] Sometimes gaslighting is a response to bad conduct on the part of the gaslighter himself. But just as often, gaslighting is a response to someone else's bad conduct. Some gaslighters have a psychological need not to "see" the bad conduct of other people who occupy particular kinds of positions in the gaslighter's psychology (e.g., authority figures, their own loved ones, people who flatter the gaslighter, or just people by whom the gaslighter wants to be liked). Some gaslighters have a psychological need not to "see" particular kinds of bad conduct irrespective of who engages in them. In both of these types of situations, the gaslighter responds by trying to radically undermine anyone who points out the bad behavior of others that they wish not to see.

C. Discrimination, Axes of Subjugation, and Gaslighting

A third common scenario for gaslighting involves situations in which the target is a member of a subjugated group and/or the subject matter to which the gaslighter is responding concerns

3. See, e.g., Girlboss, 2018 (quoting three psychologists on this point by name).

4. Psychologist Stephanie Sarkis has highlighted this context for gaslighting. See, e.g., Moore, 2019.

matters of prejudice or discrimination. This can be a version of gaslighting in response to a protest against bad conduct. But it can also be a first-order exercise in bigotry, as for instance with a domestic abuser who gaslights his spouse's efforts to stake out a form of independence that doesn't comport with his ideals of femininity.

There's nothing *necessarily* sexist or racist or classist (etc.) about gaslighting. But there's some evidence that (1) women are more frequently the targets of gaslighting than men and (2) men more often engage in gaslighting.[5] There's also reason to think that nonwhite people are more likely than white people to be the targets of gaslighting. More importantly, gaslighting is frequently, though again not necessarily, sexist and/or racist in the following ways: (3) it frequently takes place in the context of, and in response to, a protest against discriminatory conduct; (4) the forms of emotional manipulation that are employed in gaslighting sometimes rely on the target's prior internalization of sexist or racist norms; (5) when gaslighting is successful it can reinforce the very sexist or racist norms that the target was trying to resist and/or those on which the gaslighter relies in their manipulation of the target; and (6) sometimes it is some subset of those very sexist or racist norms that the gaslighter seeks to preserve through their gaslighting conduct. In short, sexist and racist norms can frame gaslighting, be employed as leverage by the gaslighter, and be reinforced when gaslighting is successful and the sexism or racism thereby gets

5. See, e.g., Stern, 2007, and Calef and Weinshel, 1981. There has recently been some dispute about these first two claims. See Dohms, 2018. Points 4, 5, and 6 are argued for in subsequent chapters herein.

hidden or erased. Gaslighting *can* involve sexism or racism or other forms of bigotry in all of these ways, some of them, or none of them.[6]

And yet gaslighting is a fiendishly brilliant tool for reinforcing racism, sexism, and other forms of systematic subjugation. As Elaine Frantz points out, "Gaslighting works so well because it does not need to give a coherent account of the world: it only needs to keep introducing enough doubt and confusion that people find it hard to look directly at the oppressions around them."[7] If you are filled with doubt about whether some act was racist and generally don't trust your abilities to make such judgments, you won't be able to see the connections between that moment and a thousand others like it. And if you don't see those connections, you won't be able to see that it is racism at which you're looking.

2. Moments in a Pattern

With these common contexts of gaslighting in mind, we can now consider some illustrative real examples of incidents involving gaslighting.

1. Simone de Beauvoir: "Day after day, and all day long, I measured myself against Sartre, and in our discussions I was simply not in his class. One morning in the Luxembourg Gardens, near the Medici fountain, I outlined for him the pluralist morality which I had

---

6. For recent discussions of racism and interpersonal gaslighting, see, e.g., Moye, 2018; Ferrentino (formerly under the moniker "Danni Starr"), 2018.

7. Frantz, 2019.

fashioned to justify the people I liked but did not wish to resemble; he ripped it to shreds. I was attached to it, because it allowed me to take my heart as the arbiter of good and evil; I struggled with him for three hours. In the end I had to admit I was beaten; besides, I had realized, in the course of our discussion, that many of my opinions were based only on prejudice, bad faith or thoughtlessness, that my reasoning was shaky and my ideas confused. *'I'm no longer sure what I think, or even if I think at all,'* I noted, completely thrown."

2. A junior academic woman is standing at the department's front desk. A male colleague passes by and slaps her on the butt. She reports the incident to another senior colleague. The second colleague responds, "Oh, he's just an old guy. Have some sympathy. It's not that big a deal." She reports it to a third colleague, who says, "Don't be so sensitive."

3. "Liz is a top-level executive . . . in her late forties. . . . Now she seems to be on the verge of reaching her goal, in line to take over the company's New York office. Then, at the last minute, someone else is brought in to take the job. Liz swallows her pride and offers to give him all the help she can. At first, the new boss seems charming and appreciative. But soon Liz starts to notice that she's being left out of important decisions and not invited to major meetings. She hears rumors that clients are being told she doesn't want to work with them anymore and has recommended that they speak to her new boss instead. When she complains to her colleagues, they look at her in bewilderment. 'But

he always praises you to the skies,' they insist. 'Why would he say such nice things if he was out to get you?' Finally, Liz confronts her boss, who has a plausible explanation for every incident. 'Look,' he says kindly at the end of the meeting. 'I think you're being way too sensitive about all this—maybe even a little paranoid. Would you like a few days off to destress?' Liz feels completely disabled. She knows she's being sabotaged—but why is she the only one who thinks so?"

4. "I started to get made fun of in random social circles, I found/got sent messages of people online saying awful things about me that were not true. I mean, how much can you say about a girl who tried to date a guy once and it didn't get very far? After a certain point and the initial rejection, I don't think I even liked him—I just wanted him to stop slandering and isolating me the way he did but he didn't want to hear me out. . . . Other students started joining in on it, I had never seen a body of people take sides and go out of their way to humiliate and shut down someone the way they treated me. My reputation had been dragged through a community I was so excited to be a part of, for reasons unknown to me till this day. My Facebook was hacked and all sorts of things were changed to compliment the gossip being spread. I tried many times to stick up for myself, but in a community of folks that toxic, anyone who spoke up against the group was deemed crazy and attention seeking. A part of me started to believe that maybe I was delusional."

5. A gay junior academic discovers a job candidate has publicly avowed antigay views. She asks to meet with

the prospective hire on a campus visit. The chair arranges the visit the one weekend he knows the junior academic will be away. In frustration, the junior academic posts copies of the university's nondiscrimination statement on department bulletin boards a few days before leaving. They disappear. She reposts them. They disappear. The chair appears at her office, torn statements in hand, and threatens her should she repost them. Later she discovers that the chair has signed a public petition asserting that it should not be regarded as a violation of disciplinary standards to fire academics in her field for being gay. She expresses grave concerns to her colleagues about what the chair has done and what he might do. They respond, "You're just acting out"; "don't be paranoid"; "that's crazy."

6. "As I entered the room, clutching a warm pile of papers, it was clear that the introductions had started and finished without me. I caught the eye of the client I worked most closely with, and to my relief she gestured to me. But just as I thought she was going to formally introduce me to the group, she dropped the clanger— 'and here is our diversity'—and swiftly returned to her conversation and her croissant.

That was my sole introduction. No name, no title. I felt myself burn up, embarrassment prickling on my skin like heavy drops of rain. When the meeting was over and the clients had left, I tearfully spoke to three senior representatives in the business (including HR) about what had happened. Not one of them could accept that anything untoward had happened. 'I'm sure she didn't mean it like that,' one remarked. 'That sounds like it was just a joke,' dismissed another. 'Oh, I heard that, I mean, it really wasn't a big deal,' said the third. And so that was the end of it; as far as they were concerned I had misunderstood, and was merely overreacting."

7. A female graduate student deals with sexual harassment, then confronts her harasser. He responds by first denying any problem, then says, "See, there wouldn't be this problem if there weren't any women in the department," and finally, "you're just a prude." She talks to another student. The second graduate student retorts, "He was just joking."

8. "Earlier this week, just before bed, an old high school debate teammate, a white man that I once loved affectionately as a younger brother, posted on my Facebook wall, "Do you have sympathy on police officers who are killed on duty?" Though we have been Facebook friends for a number of years, it has also been literal years since our last significant interaction via the site. This was a curious question that seemed forthrightly accusatory in its tone. . . . Black communities are experiencing an epidemic of severe police brutality. Even when encounters with law enforcement don't end in death, they are often shot through with disrespect from officers drunk with power. When we point this out, and when we point to case after case and story after story of inappropriate treatment, we are told that we are merely imagining it. Things aren't that bad. The cops are the good guys. *And see, they get killed, too!*"

9. "I moved out of one field of philosophy in grad school due to an overwhelming accumulation of small

incidents. . . . When I tried to describe to fellow grad students why I felt ostracized or ignored because of my gender, they would ask for examples. I would provide examples, and they would proceed through each example to 'demonstrate' why I had actually misinterpreted or overreacted to what was actually going on."

10. "In my first year of grad school (this decade) I found out that some male students had discussed a ranking of female grad students' attractiveness. I believe there was also a ranking based on 'cup size.' When I expressed to one of the offenders that the behavior was inappropriate, I was badgered for being oversensitive and philosophically interrogated for what he thought were groundless restrictions on mere conversation between male friends. It was all suggested that my concern about the list was really just a matter of my insecurity about my place on it!"[8]

As we think about these cases, it's important to consider the variety of ways these targets are characterized by their gaslighters—for example, "too sensitive," "paranoid," "crazy," "prude," or the peculiarly existentialist dismissal of "bad faith." But it's also crucial to remember that these are mere snippets from lives of people in which this sort of interaction has become pervasive. The pervasiveness of gaslighting, over a long time, often from multiple voices, is key to how and why it works.

8. The first example is from Beauvoir's *Memoirs of a Dutiful Daughter*, as quoted by Fricker 2007, 50–51. Example 3 is a summary of a patient's report in Stern, 2007, Kindle location 167–181. Example 4 is drawn from Mehta, 2018. Example 6 is drawn from Williams, 2020. Example 8 is drawn from Cooper, 2015. Examples 9 and 10 are drawn from the blog *What Is It Like to Be a Woman in Philosophy?* The remaining examples were provided to me by the targets of the gaslighting themselves.

Still, this is one of those experiences it can be difficult to grasp. If you find that's true, try this. Think about one of your worst experiences, an experience that either itself or in its effects dragged on for months. Now imagine that while you were going through that, the voices around you either flatly denied that anything worth being upset about was going on, radically minimized it, or reconceptualized the experience so that it would not be so uncomfortable (for them) to live with. You protested. The protestations were greeted with "that's crazy," "it's not a big deal," "you're overreacting." Somehow you endured. But the very fact of your survival then became woven into the rewriting of history, to confirm the minimizing and denials and later repression. ("Well, you survived, didn't you?," "It all worked out in the end," or "That was just a minor blip.") So, at no point during it did someone (or perhaps someone, but not enough, or perhaps just not the people most dear to you) look at you and confirm the reality of the horror with which you were dealing. To the contrary, they said you're crazy for being upset and oversensitive, and any difficulty you might have is "all in you." That's what gaslighting is like.

Suffering on account of it is not a sign of fragility, weakness, or an exceptionally damaged psyche; it's a sign of being human. We all need interpersonal confirmation, especially in difficult situations. And when that interpersonal confirmation is refused or deliberately thwarted, precisely in order to radically undermine someone's ability to make claims and decisions and to protest bad conduct, and their sense of having standing to do any of those things, it's gaslighting.

3

Gaslighters and Their Aims

CONSIDER SOME of the different ways in which you might respond to someone with very different views, or someone who sees a situation very differently, or someone who has desires very different from your own. You might simply note the difference or ask the other person about it with curiosity. You might wonder if you are wrong. You might search for common ground behind the disagreement. If we're talking about incommensurable desires and a question of joint action, you might try to find a fair compromise solution. If it's a close personal relationship, you might talk through with the other person any anxieties or worries raised by the differences between you. If you think the other person is mistaken about a matter of importance, you might try to persuade them to change their mind—offering reasons to see things differently, suggesting alternative perspectives, and so on. Alternatively, you might respond in one of a variety of morally disturbing ways: lying to the person to get them to see things your way on the basis of fabricated evidence; manipulating the other person into setting aside their own desires by such tried-and-true techniques as guilt-tripping, blackmail, and bribery of various sorts (emotional, financial, career, sexual, etc.); threatening the other person outright; trying to ensure that the other person's differing views or desires will constitute no obstacle to you in the pursuit of your ends by trying to make sure that no one else takes that person terribly seriously (e.g., by maliciously gossiping about them).

Or you could respond as does the gaslighter: you could try to induce in the other person the sense that their reactions, perceptions, memories, and/or beliefs are so utterly without grounds as to qualify as crazy, thereby destroying the other person's sense of having standing to issue any challenge to either your views or the way that you want things to go.

Noticing these differences reminds us, once again, how important it is to think about the gaslighter's aims—those aims are a significant part of the basis on which we distinguish gaslighting from other bad ways of acting. Yet it also highlights, albeit indirectly, how complicated is the question of why someone would choose—amid all these options—the manner of engaging with someone that involves gaslighting. On rare occasion, it may be that gaslighting someone really is the only, or best, means to a person's ends. We might imagine, for instance, that the target is socially positioned (in the broad sense, or just within a group of acquaintances or colleagues) such that they will be taken seriously and accommodated unless they are in some way genuinely losing their mind. Or we might imagine that the gaslighter has a well-earned bad reputation, perhaps especially with regard to their views about, or interactions with, the target, such that radically undermining the target in the ways characteristic of gaslighting is the only way the gaslighter can get their way, as it were, when it comes to the target.

But it's almost never like that. Not even in cases where the gaslighter fully consciously aims at destroying their target's sanity. Take Gregory, for example. The story we are given is that he is after jewels that Paula has inherited and that he knows are hidden somewhere in the attic. The attic is not an infinite space, and even Gregory (who seems rather inept at searching) would eventually find them. So here's an alternate story line: the first time Paula complains about the gaslights dimming (as they do in her bedroom every time he turns them on in the attic) he purchases a small handheld lantern. He then continues his habit of telling Paula he's going out (something she never questions at any rate) until he finds the jewels. He sells them and disappears. All that would have been a good deal easier than gaslighting Paula. Similarly, in what seem to be the first two cases referred to as instances of gaslighting in the psychological literature, the bad actors' intentions were entirely conscious. Both cases involved female spouses engaging in behavior remarkably similar to the fictional Gregory's, for the purpose of having their respective husbands committed to mental institutions. And in both cases doing so was a means to getting rid of the husband, so the woman could be with another man.[1] Divorce, to be sure, was more frowned upon in the United States in 1969 than it is in

1. Barton and Whitehead, 1969, describe these two cases, along with a third that they are unsure fits the phenomenon they want to pick out. They make no attempt to analyze the phenomenon or the motives of the actors, save to note that both women wanted to get rid of their husbands to be with other men.

the twenty-first century. But there were numerous lies the women could have told their social networks (e.g., that he was having an affair) that would have saved them from social stigma at least as much as would "my husband went insane" and would have involved considerably less trouble to make believable than was the effort required to gaslight their husbands.

This puzzle about why gaslighters choose to act as they do is, in one sense, a straightforwardly psychological issue. But it is not of *mere* psychological significance. Thinking closely about the kind of motivational psychology that leads people to engage in gaslighting serves our purposes here in three important ways. First, it will contribute to the case—a case that as I've said is being offered here cumulatively, over the whole book—that we should see gaslighting as involving specifiable aims. Second, it will allow us to further specify the gaslighter's aims. And third, there are aspects of the background motivational psychology at issue here that are morally salient. Just as it matters, morally speaking, whether someone who commits murder was motivated, say, by the desire to get away with a burglary or by seething bigotry toward an entire group, so too here the background facts about a gaslighter's motivational psychology can make a moral difference.

1. The Aims of Gaslighting—A Second Pass

Given the fact that there is this puzzle about what motivates gaslighters even when their aims are conscious and openly avowed, and the fact that it's common for gaslighting aims to be evident though not conscious, it's not surprising that the first academics to think seriously about the phenomenon were psychoanalysts. When gaslighting first became a technical term in psychoanalysis, it was understood as one form that the defensive process of projective identification could take.[2] Here's the general idea of projective identification. Someone feels something with which he is so uncomfortable that he's unable to acknowledge it. So he attributes his feelings to someone else. So far, all we have is projection, as when someone with unacknowledged anger starts fearfully wondering if others are angry with him. Or consider the familiar case of the person who has a crush he cannot bring himself to acknowledge, and so believes that the object of his crush has a crush on him. It becomes projective identification when the projector needs the other person to play along, and she obliges—in psychological terms, she introjects. One common example goes as follows: He feels anxious about his abilities, cannot tolerate the anxiety, and so does his best to expel that anxiety by producing it in someone else. If it works, what he gets is roughly "I'm not anxious, you are." Of course, he's made that the case by acting so as to produce anxiety in the other person.

There is, I'll contend, something right about this analysis of gaslighting. First, both projective identification and gaslighting involve one person creating the conditions such that their own deep anxieties are relieved in virtue of the fact that another person is manipulated into manifesting in the world that which the first person needs to see. Second, in both projective identification and gaslighting, the target is not a mere passive recipient—in projective identification, she takes in ("introjects") that which he is trying to produce in her; in gaslighting,

2. The foundational article here is Calef and Weinshel, 1981.

as we'll see (in chapters 4 and 6), the target is commonly made similarly complicit in her own undoing. Third, in both cases, other motives, other people, and other motives involving other people (conscious and not) are frequently implicated in ways to which we need to pay attention to have an apt picture of the projective identification/gaslighting.[3]

But "projective identification" doesn't seem to be quite the right terms in which to understand the underlying motives at stake in gaslighting. Canonical cases of projective identification involve one person projecting onto another something about themselves that they cannot accept, and the second person then "introjecting"—taking on, or adopting, even if only temporarily—that which has been projected onto them. It's also central to the notion of projective identification that a quality (say, an emotional state) that actually exists prior to the projective identification in one person is, through projective identification, produced or "relocated" in another person. Many paradigm cases of gaslighting don't fit the category of projective identification in either respect.

Consider, for instance, the following scenes from the movie *Pat and Mike*. Pat is an expert golfer engaged to a man, Collier,

---

3. "Textbook" cases of projective identification involve one person projecting into another something about *themselves* they cannot accept. But there are cases in which the projected state belongs to a third party. For example, a teenager experiences his parent as "controlling" but cannot allow himself to experience anger at his parent. So he reconfigures his relationship with his sibling as one in which the sibling is "bossing" him—either by reconceptualizing the siblings' reasonable behavior as bossy or by creating conditions under which the sibling will respond by in fact bossing him. Now he can "kick the dog"—that is, get angry with his sibling while avoiding dealing with his feelings about his parents' behavior.

who would rather she abandon her serious full-time career aspirations, marry him, and devote herself to wifely endeavors. That she doesn't want this for her own life threatens his personal sense of manhood. So he defensively "worries" about her golfing abilities, frequently expressing these "worries" to Pat. Pat gradually becomes anxious about her skills but perseveres and reaches the championship. She's winning. Until the final round. Then Collier shows up and makes faces of "concern"; her confidence is shaken. It all comes down to the last hole. Right before taking what should have been her final, easy shot, Pat looks up to see Collier's "worried" face. She loses. Afterward, the two have the following exchange on the train:

COLLIER: How about looking on the bright side of this for instance? Now, take this—as long as your job's out of the way, we move our date up, tie the old knot? I think you've worked long enough, done enough, don't you?

PAT [distressed]: Oh, too much. [looks down]

COLLIER [interrupting Pat]: What are you trying to prove, who you trying to lick?

PAT [determinedly, upset]: Myself. [pounds fist in air]

COLLIER: You're just the kid who can do it. [puts his leg up, his arm around the back of the seat in which she's seated, and looks at her both dubiously and patronizingly]

PAT: Collier, do you sort of, I don't think you mean to, but do you think of me as just a little woman?

COLLIER: That's right, and myself as a little man. [squeezes her shoulders like a small child]

PAT [quite distressed]: Right now I . . . I feel sort of like a flop that you're rescuing. I'm flummoxed, that's what

I am. Maybe we ought to wait until I don't feel so
carved up, so nobody.

COLLIER: Why don't you just let me take charge!

PAT [fatigued]: I have to be in charge of myself.

COLLIER: Oh what's the good of this? I mean after all, we . . .

PAT: Have to have time to think it over is all.

COLLIER: Well, just see that you don't think it under. It's
a nice long ride. Just take your time. [opens newspaper
to end conversation]

Now we've got a case that's pretty clearly in the territory of
gaslighting. Yet it's difficult to read as an instance of "projective
identification": it hardly seems like there's anything about
himself that Collier is trying to rid himself of by "relocating" it
in Pat. There's certainly some kind of defensive maneuver in
play—Collier's "worries" that Pat cannot succeed as a golfer are
a defensive cover for his own desire that she want something
for her own life that she does not. But it's not the fact that there
is such a defensive maneuver in play that makes this recognizable as an instance of gaslighting. It's recognizable as gaslighting because Collier is so clearly trying to radically undermine
Pat, and doing so through a combination of dismissing (e.g.,
"oh what's the good of that, I mean after all") and manipulating
her (especially via her trust and love).

Notably, the sense in which Pat ends up undermined isn't
just about her golfing abilities—she says she feels "carved up,"
"nobody." This kind of language is common among targets of
successful gaslighting. It's in the same category, for instance,
as Beauvoir's "I am no longer sure . . . even if I think at all." It's
language that speaks to a sense of having lost one's independent

standing as deliberator and moral agent. And, significantly, it's language that mirrors the canonical language of gaslighters. That is, gaslighters charge their targets with being crazy, oversensitive, paranoid. What these terms have in common in the context of gaslighting is that they are ways of charging someone not simply with being wrong or mistaken, but being in no condition to judge whether she is wrong or mistaken. The accusations are about the target's *basic rational and emotional competence—her ability to get facts right, to deliberate, her basic evaluative competencies and ability to react appropriately, her independent standing as deliberator and moral agent.* When gaslighting succeeds, it drives its targets crazy in the sense of deeply undermining just these aspects of their independent standing.

2. On the Difficulty of Naming Aims

So is that what gaslighters want—to undermine their targets as deliberators and moral agents? Is that their aim? Ultimately, I think something like that is right. But this is also tricky territory for various reasons, and in this section I want to walk through some of the most obvious features of these cases that might make us hesitate to attribute such aims. Doing so will bring us closer to seeing why it's in fact plausible to attribute such awful aims to gaslighters.

Let's start by thinking about gaslighters who are every bit as explicit and consciously aware of what they are doing as was the fictional Gregory.[4] Even in those cases, what the gaslight-

4. E.g., the two cases discussed in the 1969 *Lancet* piece; Bowles, 2018; Zeiderman, 2019.

ers avow as their stated aim doesn't get much more precise than "drive them crazy" (typically followed by "so that they will be institutionalized in a mental hospital"). Talk of undermining someone's standing as deliberator and moral agent is philosophically specific, and one might worry that it's more precise than that for which these gaslighters' behavior and avowed attitudes give warrant. I've offered some reason already to think such precision is plausible—it allows us to make sense of the all too close fit between the kinds of things gaslighters typically say to their targets and the condition into which successful gaslighting puts its target (think of Beauvoir's "I am no longer sure . . . if I think at all").

To get any further than this, we'll need to think more about the puzzle with which I opened this chapter—that is, the puzzle about why gaslighters choose to do what they do, when there are so often much easier ways (than driving someone crazy) of getting what they want (like acquiring hidden jewels or freedom from an unwanted romantic partner). But before we discuss that question, we need to first broaden our scope to include gaslighters whose aims are obscure to themselves.

When we speak of someone as having an "aim" in this sense, one which they do not acknowledge and of which they are not aware, we're not in the territory of explicit features of conscious deliberation but rather speaking of what will in some sense satisfy the gaslighter.[5] This is a notion of a person's hav-

---

5. Gaslighters, like everyone else, often have conflicting desires and motives and, for that reason, can be simultaneously satisfied as well as distressed when successful, just as I can be satisfied for the measure of justice accomplished when a criminal is caught at the same time that I'm sad for the pain his family will thereby endure.

ing an aim that is familiar in everyday life. We routinely attribute aims to people of which they are themselves unaware. We say that people who pick fights with loved ones just before having to spend an extended time apart are trying to make the separation easier on themselves. We accurately speak of people "trying to be the center of attention" or "being controlling" even when they sincerely disavow it. And when someone who quite obviously doesn't want to do the laundry does so begrudgingly, and all the whites end up pink as a result of a "forgotten" red sock, we call them passive-aggressive. They didn't want to do the laundry, and having turned all the whites pink they're unlikely to be asked to do it again, so it certainly looks like there's an aim that was satisfied by the inclusion of that red sock in the whites. Some of these aims may be unconscious, or preconscious, in the technical psychoanalytic sense. But ordinary usage, and the apt attribution of such aims, doesn't depend on any particular such theory of the mind.

In this sense of having an "aim," every individual gaslighter typically has multiple aims. This is true not only in the jejune sense that all people have multiple aims but also in a sense that is directly relevant to their gaslighting—gaslighting activities nearly always serve multiple aims for the gaslighter. Even Gregory does—he aims to drive Paula crazy and to run off with her hidden jewels. In Gregory's case, his aim of driving Paula crazy is instrumental to his aim of running off with her jewels. But the aims involved in gaslighting activities don't always line up in such clear means-ends ways. For example, the gaslighter who utters "that never happened" may be both trying to radically undermine his target as deliberator and moral agent and, at the same time and in a perfectly ordinary way, trying to tell himself a story about why there's nothing that happened with which he needs to deal.

It's helpful at this juncture to think about some rough categories—for heuristic purposes—into which we might sort the various aims or desires implicated in any given instance of gaslighting. In one category, closest to the psychological surface (though frequently still not conscious) are what we might call the gaslighter's target-specific aims or desires—the aims that particular gaslighters have with regard to the relevant set of interactions with a particular target. Typically, this is the aim that's exposed by asking ourselves, "What does he think he'll get if the gaslighting works?" So, for instance, Gregory thinks he'll get Paula's jewels, Collier thinks he'll get Pat to abandon her career for the sake of pursuing wifely endeavors, Sartre thinks he'll get Beauvoir sitting admiringly at his feet and gazing up in awe, Liz's boss (example 3 in chapter 2) thinks he'll get rid of Liz, and the "old high school debate teammate" (example 8 in chapter 2) thinks he won't have to acknowledge anti-Black police violence.

Such target-specific desires or aims frequently differ from what we might call a gaslighter's basic or underlying desires, which are often not specific to the target of her gaslighting. For instance, we might not implausibly suppose that Collier's most basic desire is to be the exclusive object of someone else's attention and affection. Sartre might equally plausibly be seen as driven by a need to have others prop up his fragile ego. Liz's boss (insofar as we encounter him) seems driven simply by a desire to dominate and/or maintain existing power structures while simultaneously viewing himself as kind-hearted. These are morally dark underlying aims. But that needn't be the case: some such underlying motives may be a more morally mixed case. For instance, the "old high school debate teammate," one might plausibly speculate, deeply doesn't want to be part of a world riddled with such structural racism as would make anti-Black police violence a common reality. It's not bad to *want* the world to be that way; it's profoundly morally problematic to not be willing to recognize that the world is not that way. Other underlying or basic motives that can, for particular gaslighters, get the whole train started are motives that when considered in isolation are not morally unsavory. Someone might want to see discriminatory conduct as excusable error because they have a deep need to look up to authority figures. Or they might be driven by a need to maintain harmony (or its appearance) or avoid conflict, or they may just deeply want to believe that it's all a seamless meritocracy so they can feel deserving of the credit, warmth, and welcoming they personally receive. These are psychologically problematic motives, but it's easy to imagine each of them manifesting in further downstream aims that are not at all morally problematic. The person with a need to maintain appearances of harmony might, for instance, have channeled that into diplomacy. The person with a need to believe that they participate in genuinely meritocratic systems and structures might be motivated to try to make relevant systems and structures more meritocratic than they are. And there's no reason to suppose that any individual gaslighter has only one basic or underlying motive. Their underlying motives might, for instance, be some psychologically undistinguished combination of conflict-avoidance, a desire to look up to authority figures, and a desire to preserve existing power structures.

Notice that not one of the target-specific or underlying desires I've just mentioned need depend for its satisfaction on gaslighting someone. If, for instance, Liz's boss ultimately wants to maintain existing power structures and see himself as judicious and kind, why doesn't he just ignore Liz? Or, short of that, simply end his meeting with her with what we are told are his plausible explanations for his misconduct toward her, rather than go on to suggest that she's being oversensitive and should take a few days off to destress? Similarly, if what's motivating the fellows in conversation with the junior colleague who was slapped on the butt is that they want to minimize the harm of sexual harassment (the specific aim) because they are driven by a desire to want to look up to authority figures (the underlying aim), why not just dismiss the incident with something as simple as the phrase "I don't see it that way"? Why, instead, call upon her to have sympathy for her harasser; why insist she's being "oversensitive"? If Collier wants to be the exclusive object of someone's attention and affection, why radically undermine Pat's career ambitions, rather than finding someone who doesn't have any such independent ambitions? If the person in the meeting who referred to someone with the quip "and here is our diversity" (example 6 in chapter 2) *as she walked into the room* just wanted her not to be taken seriously, why not gossip behind her back rather than to her face? Why is the old high school debate teammate even engaging with his Black acquaintance online? Or consider, finally, the person deeply motivated by a desire for harmony. While successfully gaslighting someone who objects to injustice produces some sort of harmony, there's hardly a necessary connection between having a desire for harmony and being motivated to gaslight dissenters. Why see she who objects to injustice as the person who has disrupted harmony, rather than they who have perpetrated the injustice in the first place? And even insofar as he focuses on the objector, why configure "harmony" as something that requires her total silencing (gaslighting) rather than simply ignoring or even appeasing her (either in addition to, or as opposed to, the perpetrators of the injustice)?

All of these target-specific and underlying motives (and many others besides) sometimes play a role in the psychology of specific gaslighters. Some of them are probably common. I'd speculate, for instance, that on some deep psychodynamic level a desire to preserve existing social-power structures (of the sort perhaps in play in the case of Liz's gaslighting boss) is very often in play when gaslighting occurs in response to someone's protest against discriminatory conduct. The problem is that that doesn't explain the gaslighter's behavior— there are a myriad of ways, for instance, to preserve existing oppressive structures in the face of someone's protest against them that don't involve gaslighting the one who protests. Something more has to be going on in the psychology of gaslighters to explain their behavior.

3. Explaining Gaslighters and Specifying Their Aims

One important part of the explanation here is the inability of gaslighters to tolerate even the possibility of challenge. A clinical psychoanalyst who works and writes on the subject puts it this way: "A gaslighter . . . can't tolerate the slightest challenge to the way he sees things. However he decides to explain the world to himself, that's how you must see it, too—or leave him prey to unbearable anxiety."[6] There are, unsurprisingly, variations on this theme. There can be, for instance, variations in the scope of the arenas in which he cannot tolerate disagreement. Any given gaslighter, that is, might be able to tolerate challenges to some aspects of his views (say, literature or restaurant quality) but not others (say, what qualifies as sexual harassment or discrimination). And he might be able to tolerate disagreement from some people (say, male authority figures or strangers) but not others (say, women who are his career equals).

But however wide its scope along either dimension, it is this intolerance and intense anxiety about the very possibility of disagreement that provides the first missing key in the explanation as to why gaslighters behave as they do.[7] The point I'm trying to make here is somewhat more subtle than it might at first seem. Understanding that most gaslighters deeply cannot tolerate being challenged (especially perhaps those whose aims are not conscious) provides a crucial part of the explanation for why they behave as they do. But it is also importantly *incomplete* as an explanation of gaslighting behavior, even where it does play a significant motivational role. Suppose I cannot tolerate challenges to my views about some topic. Suppose it's true as well that I feel "unbearable anxiety"—as Stern describes it—when faced with disagreement. There are various ways I might make that disagreement "go away." I might ignore it or decide

6. Stern, 2007, Kindle location 275.
7. What follows is an emendation to my 2014 view.

that the source is unreliable (that is, opt for the mode of dismissal toward the person disagreeing with me), or I might try to make sure that there's no uptake on the disagreement—that is, I might try to make sure no one else takes the disagreement seriously. None of that involves gaslighting the person who is the source of the disagreement. The gaslighter responds in a very particular way to the threat they experience in the face of disagreement: they try to get rid of the disagreement by getting rid of the disagree-er, as such, making her into instead a "crazy person" whose utterances don't qualify as disagreements.

This tells us something interesting and perhaps surprising about the gaslighter. They actually deeply care—in the sense of being invested in—what their targets think, believe, feel. Otherwise, even their being intolerant of disagreement to the point that they find it emotionally unbearable would not explain their behavior. *It is about you*, the target.

That doesn't mean that the gaslighter's investment in what their target thinks or feels is, in the colloquial sense, *personal* as opposed to impersonal. That's not the right contrast to have in mind. The relevant contrast is the difference between someone who doesn't care why the target does x (asserts x, stays silent about x, doesn't show anger, etc.), just so long as they do it, and someone who cares very much why the target does x.

Here's a real case that brings out the relevant contrast nicely. Amanda Knox was wrongly convicted of murdering her roommate after a long interrogation that she describes as an effort in gaslighting:

[My interrogators] engaged in a relentless campaign of lies & gaslighting. They isolated me and made me vulnerable. . . .

> They kept me overnight. They told me I had amnesia, that
> I was so traumatized by events I'd witnessed, that I'd re-
> pressed them. They shouted at me to remember, REMEMBER!
> They slapped me. . . . They made me feel insane. Like
> I couldn't trust my own thoughts, my own memories. I started
> to believe them that I had amnesia, that I'd witnessed
> something horrific. . . . They wrote a statement for me, a
> confused and contradictory statement, that implicated my
> boss, Patrick, and placed me at the scene of the crime. Shak-
> ing and tired and gaslit into submission, I signed it.[8]

Knox's interrogators clearly had no personal concern for her—
of the sort one might have for a friend or spouse. But in the
sense relevant for my analysis of gaslighting, it's plausible to
think that Knox's interrogators were invested in what she believed. It was *about her, about what Knox herself thought and
believed.* The police sometimes do terrible things to get people
to "confess" to things they never did. But many of those terrible, and effective, means don't involve trying to confuse the
suspect about what happened. Sometimes false confessions
are more the result of misconduct in the category of brute
coercion ("just sign this and we'll let you sleep/call your
lawyer/etc.") or simple forced choice ("sign this confession
and take this deal, or it'll be much worse for you—we'll see to
it that you're locked up for ten times as long"). Even the old
police trick of falsely claiming to have evidence of a crime
commonly can work as part of a forced-choice situation (viz.,

8. https://twitter.com/amandaknox/status/1355332022139408384. My
thanks to an anonymous referee for bringing this case, and its relevance here, to
my attention.

"well, you're telling me you weren't there, but we've got your DNA and your knife, so I don't know what to tell you . . . the prosecutor will go easier on you if you just sign this confession") The fact that Knox's interrogators chose to try to undermine her basic sense of reality rather than use simple trickery or force to get her to sign a confession suggests that they were, after all, invested in what *she* thought.

The characteristic aim of gaslighting, in other words, is interpersonal in the sense that it is a need gaslighters have of and directed toward particular persons.[9] Again, these are not the guys who roll their eyes and walk away when a woman points out that something is sexist. These are the guys who turn to that woman, insist that she's crazy, and insist that she assent in some way to the proposition that she's crazy. They don't just need the world to appear to themselves to be a certain way—they need you, the target, to see it that way.[10] But you don't. He needs this to be "just some poor old guy" he can admire, rather than a sexual harasser. You point out the sexual harassment. And because the gaslighter cannot tolerate the "slightest challenge to the way he sees things" he needs the challenge you've

9. I've been helped here by thinking through interpersonal directedness as explored in Leite, 2016.

10. The interpersonal need involved in the gaslighting aim might also be directed at different persons from those implicated in the gaslighter's underlying desires or aims. For instance, X's underlying desire is to see herself as the only "real relationship" in Y's life. For that reason, X cannot tolerate Y's relationship with Z. So X gaslights Z. If successful, Y's relationship with Z may then be configured by both X and Y as, say, "charity for 'crazy' old Z," rather than a "real relationship," thereby serving X's need to be the only "real relationship" in Y's life. Indeed, if gaslit, Z herself may come to see things in these terms. For instance, some of the behavior of the characters in the movie *Heathers* fits this general pattern.

just presented to completely disappear as a challenge. The only way for that to actually happen, *given his investment in your view of the situation*, is for you not to have the standing to issue challenges and to not see yourself as having that standing.

The central desire or aim of the gaslighter, to put it sharply, is to destroy even the possibility of disagreement—to have his sense of the world not merely confirmed but placed beyond dispute. And the only sure way to accomplish this is for there to be no source of possible disagreement—no independent, separate, deliberative perspective from which disagreement might arise. So he gaslights: he aims to destroy the possibility of disagreement by so radically undermining another person that she has nowhere left to stand from which to disagree, no standpoint from which her words might constitute genuine disagreement.

If we set this as the paradigm case of a gaslighting aim, gaslighting aims will then, and to that extent, belong to a particular family of dismissive interactions characterized as a family insofar as the parties to them fail to treat disagreements as seriously as they ought to be treated, for reasons having to do with psychological difficulties the parties have in dealing with disagreements. And some close cousins in this family may be difficult to distinguish in situ from gaslighters. There are those, for instance, who need their vision of the world socially confirmed by most, but not all. For this person, it will be enough if everyone else thinks the woman who is pointing to sexism is crazy. She won't then have social standing to dispute his views, in the ordinary sense that no one will take her challenges seriously. Notice, however, that for a person so motivated, there doesn't seem to be any motive for engaging with the person who objects to sexism. Indeed, if the aim is that everyone else think she is crazy, it may be tactically better not to speak *to* she who objects but to speak only *about* her.

The gaslighter is different because he wants and needs more than that—he wants it to actually *be* the case that *she* cannot issue genuine challenges to him. The only way to accomplish that is to gaslight her—to try to make it the case that she's left with no independent standpoint from which to issue a challenge. What he gets, and his cousin doesn't, is that *he gets to be right.* This, in my view, is the core insight of early psychoanalytic attempts to understand gaslighting in terms of projective identification, for what projective identification creates at the most general level is a situation in which one person's anxieties and needs are relieved by making external reality fit the contours of those anxieties/needs. Merely creating a situation in which everyone regards a woman as unhinged, without actually unhinging her, doesn't accomplish that.

One might worry that this characterization of the gaslighter is too strong. One respect in which my characterization may seem too sharp has to do with how we think about the relationship between some of the examples we've been talking about and the destructive aims I've claimed are characteristic of gaslighting. If we think of the paradigm case of gaslighting as one in which the gaslighter wholeheartedly, constantly, and consistently aims at the destruction their target's standing to issue challenges, it may be less than entirely clear that all of these are examples of gaslighting. This appearance is partly mitigated by remembering that these are vignettes in the lives of people for whom this sort of interaction has become pervasive when it comes to their gaslighters. A single instance of one person saying to another "that's crazy" may not appear to be—may not be—an instance of someone trying to destroy another's standing to make claims. But when that form of interaction is iterated over and over again, when counterevidence to "that's crazy" is dismissed, when nothing is treated as salient evidence for the possibility of disrupting the initial accusation, appearances shift.

Equally importantly, we also need to bear in mind that gaslighters—like the rest of us—commonly have conflicting aims/desires. In fact, we've already seen as much. I've characterized Sartre's target-specific aim, for example, as wanting Beauvoir to sit in awe of him at his feet. Satisfaction of his gaslighting desire to destroy Beauvoir's independent standing both would and would not support this more specific aim. On the one hand, the more Beauvoir's own sense of her philosophical abilities is undermined, the more likely she is to sit in awe of Sartre at his feet. On the other hand, if she really came to consistently doubt whether she can "think at all," Beauvoir would be so undermined that she wouldn't have enough sense of her own acumen left to be in awe of Sartre's abilities. A similar tension seems to hold between the general and the specific aims of the gaslighters involved in some of the other cases—such as the case of Pat and Collier.

One might, in this light, try to amend my descriptions of the aims of gaslighting so we can make a consistent whole out of the gaslighter's desires. Perhaps, one might suggest, the gaslighter typically wants to undermine his target not to the point where she loses the ability to challenge altogether but just to the point where he gets other things he wants—a woman devoted exclusively to wifely endeavors, a philosopher sitting in awe at his feet, a colleague willing to treat discriminatory conduct as though it were an exercise of justified authority. But the conflicted picture of the gaslighter strikes me as closer to the truth, at least in most cases. For one thing, attempting to reconcile at a philosopher's distance the otherwise apparently conflicting aims of the typical gaslighter problematically glosses over their destructive impulse and "unbearable anxiety" at the possibility of challenge that underwrites that impulse. By the same token, however, there is more than simply such a destructive impulse at work in most of these cases. Most gaslighters are not great evildoing caricatures of the sort Gregory is (he is, after all, a movie character). To the contrary, people who engage in gaslighting often also want to maintain a relationship, sometimes a very close relationship, with their targets.

Furthermore, keeping the fact of the gaslighter's conflicting motives in mind is often important for understanding how things look from the perspective of the *target* of gaslighting. If she's being gaslit, her gaslighter's destructive motives aren't going to be transparent to her. Yet frequently the explanation for why that's so difficult for her to see lies not solely in the clever deceptive manipulativeness of the gaslighter but also in the fact that there's something else that's often true—he does have an investment in having a relationship with his target, an investment that she can see, and that is often something that was true long before the gaslighting began.[11]

Indeed, the gaslighter's demands for assent are often simultaneously expressions of the characteristic destructive desire ("be crazy so I don't have to view myself as challenged by you")

11. See also the discussion of trust in chapter 7.

and, at the same time, expressions of a desire to maintain relations with their targets ("just go along with me on this, so we can get on with our relationship"). Think, for instance, of the urgency with which—immediately after her loss in the golf tournament—Collier tries to get Pat to agree to marry him. He wants her undermined so that she will "just let him take charge," but he also desperately wants her to assent—and to want of her own accord—to marry him (and so to have stable enough desires and will to do so). An apt description of the case, it seems to me, will simply let the tension in his motives stand as it is. And yet for all the complexities, it remains the destructive impulse that distinguishes the aims of a gaslighter: it's the intense anxiety, the target-specific and target-directed fear of challenge, and the need to destroy that very possibility that drives him.

We will see further evidence of this in the next chapter. There, in chapter 4, we turn to consideration of the typical methods and means of gaslighting. Laying bare common patterns involved in gaslighting interactions and the tools that gaslighters use is important both for getting the phenomenon properly in view and for understanding the multidimensional nature of its immorality. In addition, however, it provides further vindication of the arguments from this chapter about the gaslighter's aims. The basic structure at issue in my characterization of these core destructive aims of gaslighting—an interpersonally directed need for assent, a similarly directed intolerance for challenge or even the possibility of being challenged, and the manipulative destruction of the target's standing to issue challenge—can all be read fairly straightforwardly off the typical pattern of gaslighters' interactions with their targets.

4

The Methods and Means
of Gaslighting

IN THIS CHAPTER we'll explore in detail the typical tools and patterns of manipulation that are involved in gaslighting. There are three reasons it's important to do so. First, the tools that gaslighters use to manipulate their targets and the particular patterns of manipulation in which they prototypically engage are part of what makes gaslighting a recognizably distinct phenomenon. Guilt-tripping someone and "playing damsel in distress" are both ways of manipulating someone, but they involve recognizably different patterns of conduct and tools of manipulation—hence the different colloquialisms by which we name these forms of manipulative conduct. So too gaslighting involves not only distinctive aims (as we saw in chapter 3) but also distinctive patterns of manipulative conduct. Second, the particular patterns of manipulative conduct that gaslighters engage in, and the particular tools they characteristically use to do so, both constitute important dimensions of the immorality of gaslighting: *how* one achieves a deeply morally wrong aim matters in the evaluation of one's conduct. Third, as we will see, there's a peculiarly awful sort of "fit" between, on the one hand, the paradigmatic tools and techniques of gaslighters and, on the other, their aims. Gaslighters aim to fundamentally undermine their targets as deliberators and moral agents. And the particular tools gaslighters use in pursuit of that aim involve unavoidably fundamental aspects of our lives as deliberators and moral agents.

1. The Big Picture

Ordinary attempts at manipulation like "guilt-tripping" sometimes work, sometimes don't, and sometimes work only partially. Many attempts to gaslight similarly fail. What's surprising is that they ever succeed. Consider the vast difference between (1) being manipulated into going to a movie one would rather not see and (2) being manipulated into losing one's sense of standing as an independent moral agent and deliberator, as well as having the skills constitutive of one's moral agency and deliberative abilities themselves deeply undermined. How could something as enormous, as psychologically devastating as the latter ever happen as a result of manipulative interactions?

The movie *Gaslight* gives us two overlapping answers to that question—one that portrays our protagonist, Paula, as damaged and vulnerable on account of early childhood trauma and a second story that focuses on the various forms of leverage her husband, Gregory, uses to manipulate her, and the patterns of manipulation by which he attempts to drive her insane. In a sense, I think the movie is right to have both sides of the "how it happens" story in play. But the movie's way of weaving together these two threads is problematic on two counts. First, while it's true that some people are more vulnerable than others to being gaslit, no one is immune, and there can be false comfort gained by fixating on Paula's peculiar vulnerability. Moreover, Paula's special vulnerability doesn't lessen Gregory's blameworthiness. If anything, it ought to intensify our blame. If a mugger decides to target me because I'm walking slowly with a cast on a broken leg, we might well think he's worse for targeting me because I'm especially vulnerable; we certainly don't say part of the blame lies on me for having a broken leg.

And yet, while all of this is true, and while gaslighting is, in every relevant moral sense, something done *to* the target, it is nevertheless true that *what* is done to the target is the result of their *interactions* with the gaslighter. That is, the target of gaslighting is not *simply* a passive recipient of the gaslighter's ill will and conduct in the way someone would be if a person snuck up behind them and hit them over the head with a rock. Instead, as we'll see, there's an important sense in which targets of gaslighting are made active participants in their own undoing. In that sense, the movie was right to draw our attention to the Paula side of the gaslighting interaction in painting its narrative of how she comes to be gaslit.

The other part of the story of how gaslighting works is, of course, what the gaslighter does—their typical patterns of manipulative conduct, and the tools they paradigmatically use in order to manipulate their targets. In fact, I'll suggest, there's a peculiarly awful fit between the gaslighter's aims and the tools they employ in gaslighting. Perhaps most importantly, they are precisely the tools that are best suited to induce the target of gaslighting to turn against herself in the ways she must if her deliberative capacities and moral agency are to be undermined in the ways at which the gaslighter aims.

2. Paula's Inescapable Dilemma

Gaslighting is accomplished through manipulative means that leave its target rightly sensing in the aftermath that she has been turned against herself. In this respect, gaslighting has much in common with the mechanisms that David Sussman argues are paradigmatic of torture.[1] What's especially awful about torture, on Sussman's account, is that a victim's will is turned against itself; she is made to feel, for instance, that at every moment there is something she could do to stop it, to escape, and that false feeling of escapability becomes itself part of the torture. A very similar point can be made about gaslighting—the targets of gaslighting have their basic reflective processes, their affective capacities, and sometimes even their character turned against them in the service of their own destruction. They are *blamelessly* active, but nevertheless still active, in the process. Here's Sussman elucidating the point with regard to torture:

> I do not regard the wrong of torture as just disregarding, thwarting or undermining the victim's capacities for rational self-governance. Instead, I argue that torture forces a victim into the position of colluding against himself through his own affects and emotions, so that he experiences himself as

1. Sussman, 2005.

simultaneously powerless and yet actively complicit in his own violation. (4)

Something very roughly like this takes place even in quite ordinary forms of manipulation. Consider, for example, the guilt trip. A successful guilt trip involves manipulating someone into feeling unwarranted guilt, typically in order to get them to do something. A guilt trip works better if the person who feels guilty doesn't realize that their guilt is the unwarranted result of manipulation. But even if one does realize one is being manipulated, guilt-tripping can be effective. In that latter case, one is in a position very much like Sussman describes—experiencing oneself as simultaneously powerless (overwhelmed by guilt that one recognizes as unwarranted) and yet actively complicit (following that guilt where it leads in action).

But if we follow Sussman's account of torture, the role of the target's complicitly therein differs from that which is involved in the ordinary guilt trip in three key respects. First, having a sense that one is complicit in one's ill treatment is a defining characteristic of torture: that's a central part of what's torturous about it. In contrast, one can be successfully guilt-tripped without any sense that that's happened, let alone feeling complicit in it. Second, on Sussman's account, in torture the central motivating disposition—that which one is induced to experience, and which bids one to act to make the torture stop (though it's impossible)—is pain (as opposed, obviously, to the guilt involved in the guilt trip).[2] And third, torture involves iterated action, whereas being guilt-tripped canonically does not.

2. See Sussman, 2005, 20.

The target of gaslighting ends up both *being* and *feeling* complicit in her own undoing in ways that differ from both guilt trips and torture. First, some aspects of the experience of being brought to collude against oneself are not first-personally transparent in gaslighting in the way they can be in guilt-tripping or torture. The victim of torture can know that her pain is leading her to talk and act as though she has an escape, even as she knows perfectly well from a perspective outside her pain (yet still very much her own perspective) that there is no such escape: "Please, I'll tell you whatever you want, just stop!" Similarly, someone who has been guilt-tripped can recognize that she was manipulated into feeling guilty and feel complicit in part precisely because she knows was manipulated into feeling guilty and acting on that guilt. ("I know I have no reason to do this for her; she's guilt tripped me into it and I feel unable to stop myself.") In paradigm cases of gaslighting, on the other hand, one ends up feeling not complicit in someone else's wrongdoing but *at fault*. To see oneself as *complicit* in the gaslighters misconduct, one would have to see it for what it is—to see them as aiming at radically undermining you as deliberator and moral agent. But it's in the very nature of the ways in which the target of gaslighting is brought to collude against herself (as we'll see shortly) that if she did recognize her gaslighter's intentions, she couldn't be brought to collude against herself in that way. Only in the aftermath, in the slow recovery from having been gaslit, can one see that one was complicit in one's own undoing, rather than simply at fault for it.

This first difference among the tortured, the guilt-tripped, and the gaslit—a difference in their sense of their own role in their suffering—is closely related to a second, namely, a difference in the agent-states most centrally implicated in their having been brought to collude against themselves. For the person who has been guilt-tripped, it's their guilt; for the tortured—as Sussman notes—it's their pain.[3] In each of these cases, the state (guilt/pain) is brought about through the bad conduct of the wrong-doer (the manipulator/torturer), but in experiencing the state as her own and being motivated by it, the target is induced to collude against herself. In gaslighting, by contrast, it's centrally the *processes* by which one routinely forms apt beliefs, doubts, and reactive responses, and one's *motivationally organizing* desires and affections that are made use of by the gaslighter and put one in a position of colluding against oneself.

To see this last point at work, and to get a sense of why someone who has been gaslit will paradigmatically see herself not as having colluded with her tormentor but as at fault for her own undoing, we need consider only a few simple examples. (Further details of how some of this works will come to light as we consider particular tools that gaslighters use as manipulative leverage in section 3.) We can start by thinking about the ways in which the phrase "that's crazy" is deployed in gaslighting efforts. This phrase is typically spoken to the target with the expectation of some kind of response. The implied underlying charge is that the target herself is crazy. The phrase, however, gives the appearance of two avenues of escape for the target from that underlying charge. On one apparent escape route, if only she agrees that it is "crazy" to think x, it seems, then she can escape the charge that *she* herself is

3. See Sussman, 2005, 20.

crazy. On the other apparent escape route, "that's crazy" looks like a charge that can be *answered* with counterevidence. And so it is that the target, who after all would not have uttered the thing her gaslighter has declared crazy if she thought it so, finds herself using her reflective capacities to adduce counterevidence. "Well," she says, "I'm not the only one who thinks this is what's going on. So does this other person." Or, "look, here's evidence that precisely that happened."[4] The problem is that the appearance of a conversation, of a way to escape the gaslighter's underlying charge that you, the person who is being gaslit, are crazy was all along a mere appearance (appearance cultivated, of course, by the gaslighter). No counterevidence will be treated as such. We know what happens next; "he thinks so too" will simply be met with "well then, he's crazy too." "Here's evidence" will be met with purported reasons the evidence doesn't qualify as such. In the context of gaslighting, active use of one's own reflective capacities becomes, in such ways, part of the story of how one's deliberative capacities are fundamentally undermined. At each step, it *looks like* one is being called on to engage in an ordinary exchange of offering evidence and shared reasoning. But the more one proceeds in what in any other context would be the appropriate way to proceed—by reasoning, by offering evidence—the more one will be led by the gaslighter to doubt whether one is even capable of recognizing what qualifies as either good evidence or reasoning. Until, that is, one ends up like Beauvoir, "*no longer sure what I think, or even if I think at all.*"

4. Exchanges with the structure of these two examples have been shared with me by multiple targets of gaslighting.

Notice how vividly our two main points about the target's complicitly in gaslighting are on display here. At each step it is the target's use of her reflective capacities, deployed in ways that would be perfectly appropriate outside a gaslighting context, that draws her further toward her own undoing. It's unsurprising that targets end up feeling responsible in this context for their own suffering: the setup (by the gaslighter) is designed for precisely that, to make her feel so acutely that she's failing to reason correctly that even the basic confidence she needs to actually reason well begins to elude her (see also discussion in chapter 1 on this). But if she recognized, at any stage, what her gaslighter was up to—that he was in fact trying to undermine her as deliberator and moral agent—she'd no longer see these interactions as genuine searches for good reasons, good reasoning, and solid evidence and give up the attempt to adduce such. She wouldn't then be drawn in (any further) to the gaslighting snare. That's why, as noted earlier, someone who is *being gaslit* doesn't see herself as complicit at the time. That would require her to recognize what the gaslighter is up to, and that's something she can recognize only in the aftermath and recovery from gaslighting.

In some cases, the target's loves, empathetic capacities, or life-organizing projects are used as weapons against her in a similar fashion. In those cases, the target is induced by the gaslighter to employ the affective and reflective processes that are bound up with motivationally organizing dispositions (e.g., loving dispositions or significant life projects) in ways that are radically self-undermining. Think, for instance, of Collier and Pat, taking seriously the thought that Pat *loves* Collier and takes herself to be in a *loving relationship* with him. In the normal course of things, part of what that will involve is Pat taking it for granted that her beloved has her own interests at heart. Of course, a sensible person guided by a mature and psychologically healthy love will not assume their beloved infallible (morally or otherwise), and so will not assume that their beloved will always make accurate assessments about what's in one's interest, nor assume that their beloved will infallibly act for the sake of those interests even when they correctly assess what they are. But part of what taking oneself to be in a loving relationship means is that the assumption that one's beloved has one's interests at heart is so bedrock that it makes it unimaginable—or nearly so—that one's beloved would aim at one's fundamental undoing. Moreover, being in a loving relationship gives one reason to give one's beloved a bit more credence (than a stranger) when it comes to their views about what is in one's interest. After all, they know one better than many, and being in a loving relationship involves their having disinterested investment in your welfare.[5] When Collier raises doubts with Pat about her abilities and career plans—the steel blades of gaslighting firmly disguised in loving tones and cotton beds of ostensive concern for her—Pat's love for him will frame how she engages with those doubts. The resulting internalizations will not be a matter of her passively

---

5. We don't have reason to afford our loved ones' views more credence *in general*. Part of what we come to know about our beloved is the arenas in which they are especially *unreliable* judges. Failure or refusal to acknowledge that is a failure to love the person for who they are (rather than idealization). This is different because what's at issue is what is in one's interest, and if one's beloved is especially bad at judging *that*, they're going to be especially bad at loving since a crucial part of loving well is acting for the sake of the beloved's interest.

absorbing Collier's perspective but rather precisely the kind of active engagement with Collier's views that we should expect of Pat given her love for him and her reasonable presumption that they are in a loving relationship with one another.

We'll take an even closer look at the ways in which love and other significant reflective and affective capacities get used as tools by gaslighters in the next section. Here the central point I wish to emphasize is that gaslighters use such tools in ways that implicate the target as an active participant in her own undoing.

3. The Gaslighter's Toolbox

Almost anything *could* be used as a means of gaslighting. And any of the tools that are used for gaslighting can be used in other ways, for the sake of other ends. But there is a recognizably common set of manipulative tools used by gaslighters and, as we'll see, reasons that these are the common tools of gaslighters. In this section, I talk about how each of these everyday features of our lives and psychology gets used as a tool of gaslighting.

First, however, a couple of remarks about how I think we should understand (as a general matter) the relationship between these common tools of gaslighting and the oppressive social structures within the context of which gaslighting so often takes place. Every tool discussed in this section is especially efficient as a means of gaslighting insofar as it is used in the context of already existing power inequities, by a person with (in whatever is the relevant sense) more power. The reasons for this will be obvious when we take a closer look at how each is used as a means for gaslighting. The power inequities in question can be small-scale structural power inequities like the relation of employee to employer, larger institutional structures like the relation between police and suspect (recall the Amanda Knox example from chapter 3), or more complicated, deeper, and still broader structural inequities such as those implicated in our interactions on account of prejudicial social norms (like sexism). They can also involve more intimate, personal inequities of power—if, for instance, one person has what is colloquially called a "fear of abandonment" (as does Paula in *Gaslight*), her loved ones then have a tool for manipulation she does not hold over them; it's a relational power inequity. And there can be situational power inequities as well; when, for instance, one person is particularly emotionally vulnerable because of circumstances, the withdrawal of affection by her beloved would cause much greater harm to her than were it the other way around (think, for instance, of Collier's withdrawal from Pat just after she's lost the tournament).

At this level of analysis, social-structural inequities— sexism, racism, classism, and so forth—are important factors for understanding how gaslighting works, but not important in an essentially different way from other forms of power inequity, including very personal ones such as the vulnerabilities created by personal relational fears. Even so, however, this basic fact—that the tools of gaslighting are more efficient insofar as they're used in the context of some power inequity—does help explain the fact, now often noted in popular press discussions, that members of marginalized communities seem disproportionately targeted by gaslighting.

Yet there is also, as we'll see, one way in which members of marginalized communities are differentially situated vis-à-vis gaslighting that strikes me as a difference in kind rather than degree (or at least near enough so). The difference is this: certain prejudicial social tropes—like women are hysterical and overly emotional, Black folk are irrationally angry, those in lower socioeconomic rungs are ignorant and slow-witted—as well as certain discriminatory social norms—like women have more cause to doubt themselves than men, Black women should be especially strong/invulnerable—are used as tools of gaslighting, in ways they simply cannot be used against people who are not members of the relevant communities. In this way, oppressive social structures can play an extremely significant role in gaslighting—though the gaslighting is not something the social structures do but something *people* do with those social structures.

A. *Trust*

Trust occupies a special place in the gaslighter's toolbox partly because it is an inextricable aspect of so many other features of the interpersonal situation that can be weaponized by gaslighters—such as questions of authority in relatively formal relationships or love in close personal relationships. But even aside from this, there are features of trust that make it an especially apt and dangerous tool of gaslighters. In fact, I've come to think that the question of exactly how the gaslighter uses their target's trust as a manipulative weapon and just what that does to the target of gaslighting is so revealing (about both gaslighting and trust) that it deserves separate treatment.

That's chapter 7. Here I want simply to emphasize the easy-to-miss ubiquity of trust as a tool in gaslighting. There are two reasons this is easy to miss. First, when thinking about trust, we tend to focus on relatively close relationships. But there is literally no relationship, not the most formal nor most casual, that does not depend on trust, and when it comes to gaslighting, it's the *necessity* of trust that matters at least as much as the depth of trust. Second, when thinking about infractions of trust, we tend to think about the sort that can in a single instant break the relationship at issue. But because the efficacy of the gaslighter's efforts requires a *pattern* in which their abuses of trust are not seen as such (or, at least, in which the target is not confident that the incidents involved violations of trust), the particular infractions of trust and/or manipulations of it involved in gaslighting tend to be comparatively small-scale. Both of these points are made vivid by any of the workplace examples from chapter 2. Consider the example that begins with a woman being called over to join a working group by the client who refers to her as "our diversity." The language the author uses to describe the incident tells us that (and in what way) this was already experienced as an infraction of trust, namely, "I caught the eye of the client I worked most closely with, and to my relief she gestured to me. But just as I thought she was going to formally introduce me to the group, she dropped the clanger—'and here is our diversity.'" The denials that anything untoward had happened that followed on this incident—including by HR—exploited that fracture in trust (rather than dealt with it) to undermine *the person* who was referred to as "our diversity" (e.g., "I'm sure she didn't mean it like that"). The forms of trust being violated here—trust that colleagues won't openly say denigrating things when one joins them to work in a perfectly ordinary work setting, trust that one's complaints to HR will not be immediately brushed off without being given any consideration—are forms of trust without which a workplace cannot function. That the target of gaslighting in this case (and other similar cases) trusted her colleagues in ways that made it possible for them to exploit that trust in order to gaslight her says nothing more about her personally than that she was trying to do her job.

B. "I Might Be Wrong"

There are a variety of defeasible assumptions we make—and which we must make—in order to deliberate and to converse with others about even the most everyday matters. These defeasible assumptions include, significantly, the presumption that we are all not only fallible in our reasoning, perceptions, and memories but sometimes, in fact, wrong. We may not have any reason to doubt ourselves in a given case absent being presented with good reason for doubt. But we do not need any particular philosophical theory to see that the person who either really views themselves as infallible or else never manages to go from the thought that they are fallible to actively doubting one of their beliefs, bits of reasoning, perceptions, or memories will be neither a reasonable nor a (morally) good person. So too, there are both moral and intellectual virtues and vices of self-doubt: excesses of over-self-confidence and dogmatism, and deficits of being indecisive, diffident, and always second-guessing oneself. The gaslighter exploits all of this, turning his target's recognition of the fact that the willingness to entertain the possibility "I might be wrong" is a necessary feature of interactions between people and a crucial part of an epistemically and morally good-enough life, into a weapon against her in order to try to undermine the very possibility of the target's participating in genuine interpersonal interaction. (After all, only individuals with standing as deliberators and moral agents can engage in interpersonal interactions.)

We see this weapon of gaslighting in play in the use of many of the phrases so recognizably associated with it: "that didn't happen," "there's no pattern," "you're being paranoid," and "you're being oversensitive." All of these phrases call on the person to whom they're addressed to question her memories, perceptions, interpretations, deliberations. Sometimes that's perfectly appropriate. But when deployed by gaslighters, these phrases are meant, over time and through reiteration, to gradually induce the target to see herself as deliberatively and evaluatively incompetent with respect to whatever may be the arena at issue. And one cannot come to regard oneself as genuinely incompetent in one of these ways (as seeing patterns where there are not, as being very worried about matters not at all the proper object of concern, as experiencing wounds to one's sense of basic dignity or hurt feelings where unwarranted) without actually *becoming* to some degree actually less competent. Think, for instance, of what it would be like to come to view oneself as someone who is always seeing patterns of conduct where there aren't any. Accurately discerning such patterns involves, among other things, remembering events, considering what they have in common and asking oneself whether those apparent links have more to do with what one is bringing to the interpretation of the events or else more to do with the conduct of the other people involved, and so on. But those are activities one will be much less likely to engage in if one has come to see oneself as someone who perceives patterns where there aren't any—one might, in fact, actively try *not* to engage in such activities (erroneously) for the sake of reducing what one takes to be one's tendency to see patterns where there aren't any. Even something as simple as "remembering" (in the ordinary conscious sense) can be undermined by one's sense that one doesn't remember well. Suppose I've been gaslit into doubting my own ability to accurately remember events. Now you tell me I've done something I have no recollection of doing. All the things one would ordinarily do to figure out whether the accusation is true—like retracing one's steps or thoughts or trying to remember other details surrounding the alleged event—are activities that one will regard as pointless to the extent that one has come to see one's memory as dangerously unreliable. If my memory is *that* unreliable, why would I remember events surrounding the alleged one any better than the event it's alleged I've forgotten?

A number of other standard gaslighting tactics rely significantly on the target's willingness to actively entertain the possibility that she might be wrong. Here I want to mention just one example of such a tactic—shifting goalposts. In this context, "shifting goalposts" refers to changing midstream the criteria of what would count as success (think of some of the work-related examples) or as adequate evidence (in, for instance, cases of discrimination) precisely so that the target can never qualify as succeeding or having adduced adequate evidence. The brilliance of the shifting goalpost tactic, as a tool of gaslighting, lies in two features. First, it is executed over fairly long stretches of time, thereby making it more difficult for the target to be confident in her memories of criteria previously adduced by her gaslighter, and more difficult to adduce evidence that such were the criteria (for success or adequate evidence). The second bit of brilliance about this tactic is the ways in which it is part of shifting goalposts that it holds out the (false) promise that the target could, eventually, satisfy the gaslighter or meet some criteria necessary for getting her concerns addressed. (Here we see themes from the first section of this chapter intersecting with the gaslighter's choice of tools.) So the target is told, for instance, that she is being "oversensitive" and "paranoid" to think that her boss's sexist or racist or heterosexist remarks are sufficient reason for anyone to take action or for her to worry about what the boss will do next, but that if the boss were to violate some (further) policy, that would be cause for alarm and action. Violating some (further) policy then becomes the new goalpost, that is, criterion for justified alarm and action. And then the boss violates that (further) policy, and the gaslighter assures his target that she's misremembering, and if he (the gaslighter) said something that sounded like saying that mere violation of *that* policy would be cause for alarm, really what he meant was that a policy violation of thus and such *other* sort would be enough to trigger alarm. And on and on. The alarm will never sound.

C. Isolation

"Let all the powers and elements of nature conspire to serve and obey one man. Let the sun rise and set at his command," says Hume. "He will still be miserable, till you give him some one person at least, with whom he may share his happiness, and whose esteem and friendship he may enjoy" (T 2.2.5.15, SBN 362–363).[6] This jejune fact of human social interdependence, not only as a practical matter but emotionally, is nearly always exploited by gaslighters. They isolate their targets both literally (think of Gregory insisting to Paula that she's too unwell to go to her friends' party, or his staging the event so that she seems so unstable that they don't seek her company or conversation, or consider the isolating effects of being the colleague who enters a room only to be referred to as "our diversity" by someone formerly trusted) and metaphorically (think of Collier convincing Pat that only he, in spite of her success to date, is to be trusted when it comes to assessments of her golfing abilities). There's nothing mysterious about how isolation works as a tool of gaslighting—being isolated, literally and/or metaphorically, makes the target acutely vulnerable to the gaslighter's manipulations directly and indirectly. It does so directly insofar as it deprives the target of alternative sources of information, feedback about her own views, interpersonal confirmation, and "reality-checks" in the colloquial sense. It does so indirectly in that isolation—as Hume notes—makes perfectly healthy people miserable, and being miserable makes one emotionally vulnerable in further ways the gaslighter can exploit.

D. Love

We noted already in section 2 the fact that gaslighters often use love as a tool in gaslighting. Here are four ways they do so. First, as we've seen, being in a loving relationship with someone, ceteris paribus, plausibly gives us reason to give their

6. Hume, 1992, 362–363.

views about what is in our interest a little extra credence. We needn't go very far in this direction to see how this can become a gaslighting tool. Suppose love simply gives one reason to consider claims that concern one's own well-being further than one would otherwise. Then, when he says "you're paranoid," there's the moment to wonder, to second-guess oneself. Loving someone also involves wanting to be with the beloved, and wanting the beloved to want to be with you. In this way, it's built into the structure of loving someone that their expressing a desire not to be around you is experienced (absent further explanation) as a fracture, however small, in love. And that too gives the gaslighter a tool. Think of the moment that Collier opens the newspaper. Or consider the way in which the phrase "I'll just give you some space" can function simultaneously as a dismissal ("you're so nuts I don't want to hear you") and a threat ("continue this way and I will disappear"). Third, we want our beloveds to think well of us. To say to someone who loves you "you're crazy" is not only to condemn but also to thereby threaten one of the basic desires involved in loving.[7] Finally, loving someone involves wanting them to fare well. The evident distress on a gaslighter's face as he says, for instance, "oh have some sympathy for the guy" isn't just about "the guy": to the extent the gaslighter is distressed, and one wants people whom one loves not to be distressed, one will want to relieve his distress.

7. Some things gaslighters characteristically say leverage love more subtly. It's been pointed out to me by a psychologist, for instance, that the remark "it would be the same anywhere else" is very much like the sort of thing batterers say, viz., "no one else would treat you any differently."

E. Empathy

Our empathetic abilities can also be drawn into the service of gaslighting. Consider the junior colleague (chapter 2) who is implored to have sympathy for the guy who slapped her on the butt. Or the Black woman (chapter 2) who was pointedly asked whether she had any sympathy for the police in response to her protests against anti-Black police violence. It's possible to resist a call for empathy as outrageous. But we shouldn't underestimate the cumulative effect of social forces that heighten the possibility of empathy being leveraged in gaslighting. In many of these situations, the gaslighters are people with whom one interacts regularly and with whom one has some practical need to get along. Those two factors together facilitate empathy and make its pull harder to resist. A particular situation may be an inappropriate occasion for empathy, but if one needs to get along with the gaslighter, it's very difficult to cease empathizing or sympathizing with him altogether (or third parties with whom the gaslighter calls on one to empathize). And in this latter respect, power dynamics are a factor in the efficacy of gaslighting appeals to empathy in a very particular ways, with differential impacts on marginalized communities. First there is the simple fact that people with less power have greater need, as a practical matter, to get along with those who have relevantly more power than vice versa. Second, as Gloria Steinem reminded us long ago, precisely because those with relatively less power (e.g., secretary vs. boss) have greater need to "get along," they also tend to know more, in greater detail, about those who have relevant forms of power over them.[8] And as David Hume taught us even longer ago, the more specific an idea we can have of what it is that another person is thinking or feeling, the easier it is to empathize with them (and commensurately more difficult to resist what naturally become thereby our habits of empathizing).[9] For women in particular, there's yet another reason to expect that appeals to empathy will be an effective tool for gaslighters, namely, the fact that the familiar sexist trope that women are and should be more empathetic than men is alive and thriving in all of us. As Cordelia Fine notes, while women and men do not generally score meaningfully differently on tests for empathetic abilities, after being reminded of this trope, women's empathetic abilities suddenly increase.[10] And you get similar effects just by gender priming, by, for instance, having women tick a box that says "female"

8. Steinem, 1995, 221.

9. See *Treatise* 2.1.11 ("Of the Love of Fame"). Hume uses the word "sympathy" in this context: the word "empathy" is a later nineteenth-century invention. This is an aspect of Hume's philosophical psychology I've highlighted in published work. See Abramson, 1999. It's a lesson that advertisers learn over and over again as well. See, e.g., Gharib, 2015.

10. Fine, 2010. Note that because empathy can be "triggered" by gender priming in this way, it's especially effective as a gaslighting tool against women targets, irrespective of with whom those women targets are thereby being induced to empathize. A gaslighter might, for instance, aim to induce a woman to empathize inappropriately with another woman. Imagine, for instance, a workplace situation in which the boss is doling out favors to an attractive young woman playing "damsel in distress," and another woman objects to the unfairness. It's all too easy to imagine the boss trying to manipulate (perhaps even as part of a gaslighting effort) the objecting woman by appealing to her to "have some sympathy" for her colleague. (Scenes like this are common tropes in movies that feature older female leads or female leads we're not supposed to read as beautiful.)

before taking an empathy test. Many of the situations in which women are the targets of gaslighting also include obvious gender priming, say because the subject of the gaslighting involves sexism (e.g., the woman is protesting against sexism).

F. Practical Consequences as Manipulative Leverage

The practical consequences of trying to resist being undermined by a gaslighter can be momentous. For instance, in one of our chapter 2 examples, Liz's job is clearly at stake. And her boss has framed matters in a particular way—she's "too sensitive" and "a little paranoid" and should "take a few days off to destress." Anything short of agreeing to this will amount to disagreement with the basic framework of a boss who has shown himself more than willing to act without justification against her professional interests. Liz could try to act as though she assents to her boss's framework, while privately withholding assent. But that's not an easy feat to pull off, for reasons that have been familiar since at least Hochschild's exploration of the ways in which emotional management can be a job requirement in *The Managed Heart*.[11] One of Hochschild's examples involves flight attendants. Their job requires appearing happy and agreeable. But flight attendants quickly learn that passengers are adept at picking up on "strained or forced smiles" and so learn to actually be happy in order to appear happy.[12] Liz's situation is not

11. Here "managing" means something in the territory of what Strawson had in mind when he spoke of the standpoint from which we regard another as an "object for treatment and management."

12. Hochschild, 1983. See, e.g., Kindle locations 154–156, 179–182, 225.

wholly dissimilar—her job depends on her appearing to assent to the view that she is "too sensitive" and "maybe a little paranoid," and her boss is at least as likely to pick up on false appearances as passengers on an airplane—presumably more so, given that he interacts with her every day. In terms of job security, Liz might well be better off if she did regard herself as too sensitive. But if she reaches that point, she's been gaslit.

G. Authority and Purported Authority

Authority and purported authority also often give gaslighters manipulative leverage. First, people in actual positions of authority can use it as leverage to demand they be treated with unjustified degrees of credence. For instance, the authority of our employers gives us reason to give their views a little bit more credence over a subset of employee-related matters. If a junior faculty member's department mentor says, "Here's a good way to go about getting this done," her authority as his department mentor gives her reason to give that more credence, and that's so even if the position of department mentor and the authority thereof are derivative of presumptions of special competence with regard to, say, departmental matters. The line between cases of such justified exercises of authority and concomitant expectations of being given a little extra credence and cases where employment-related authority has overstepped its bounds is easily blurred. Gaslighters can exploit that fact. Second, there is the purported authority of the crowd, what psychologists sometimes call the "normalizing" effect of multiple voices. That's one reason why it's significant that many examples of gaslighting involve multiple gaslighters. The voice of many people is a great deal more difficult to ignore than that of one person.[13] And a reasonable person, surrounded by what otherwise seem to be reasonable people, who are in one voice telling her that she's overreacting, is not unreasonable for treating that aggregative voice with a little extra credence.

H. Stereotypes and Social Tropes

I sketched the outlines of some of the ways in which stereotypes and social tropes are used as tools by gaslighters at the beginning of this section. To understand in greater detail how such tropes can be used by gaslighters, it can be helpful to consider, by way of analogy, a common experience with familial labels or roles. There's the child who gets labeled "the smart one," another "the peace maker," another "the lazy one," another "the runaway," another "the problem child." Even if we consciously reject whatever may be our familial name tag, the invocation of that tag will have effects on us that it will not have if invoked with respect to another family member. Telling an adult who was once labeled "the problem child" that he's "causing problems" will have a different effect on him—be apt to appear to him more plausible as a going hypothesis—than saying the

13. Experiments on conformity effects support this hypothesis, notably Asch (1956). Thanks to Kirk Ludwig for bringing this to my attention. He also pointed out that follow-up experiments indicate that even one dissenter reduces the pleasure of conformity significantly (see Morris and Miller, 1975). The lesson Kirk drew is that as a matter of practical advice, if you see gaslighting, protest. Another darker lesson might be drawn—given the pleasures of conformity, and the fact that those pleasures are significantly reduced by even one dissenter, it is unsurprising that people so often go along with (if not participate in) the gaslighting of dissenters.

same thing to an adult not raised with that label. The former is primed to see himself in those terms, whereas the latter is not. Even if the adult who was once labeled "the problem child" rejects that label and thinks it was never apt, he's substantially more likely to react as though it were plausible (feeling, for instance, its pull as a self-description) than the adult who was never so labeled by their family of origin. The stereotypes and social tropes that are aspects of oppressive social structures—racism, sexism, classism, heterosexism—often work on us in roughly the same way; those subject to those stereotypes are primed to see themselves in those terms. The fact that some of us are wired by oppressive social systems to be prone to understand ourselves in terms of various stereotypes can then be made use of by gaslighters in one of three ways. First, the stereotype can be such that if successfully activated the disposition thereby prompted can be used as a tool in gaslighting. We've already seen one example of this, namely, the ways in which gender priming heightens women's empathetic abilities (on account of the stereotype that women are and ought to be more empathetic), and appeals to heightened empathy then get used as a means of gaslighting. A second, indirect, way in which stereotypes and oppressive social norms can be used by gaslighters is as tools for deflecting scrutiny from their own conduct. So, for example, "Even if he is trying to do that, you're not so weak as to fall for it are you?"—said to a Black woman, implicitly invoking the stereotype of the "strong Black woman." Or, "Come on, I'm sure you're smart enough to find a way to deal with this without me going nuclear and contacting HR" said to the East Asian employee, implicitly invoking the stereotype of the "clever" East Asian as a way of deflecting attention away from the refusal to act on a complaint of discrimination. Or,

"Huh, I guess this is just one of those situations I learned how to handle by talking to people rather than going all formal with official complaints and such; I should remember that not everyone had those privileges growing up" said to someone from a working-class background, implicitly invoking stereotypes of lower socioeconomic classes as ignorant, crude, and slow-minded, and again doing so as a way of deflecting attention away from a failure to take adequate action against discrimination. Third, oppressive social norms and stereotypes can be used more directly by the gaslighter as tools for inducing the target to see herself as unhinged, crazy, lacking basic abilities (and hence standing) as deliberator and moral agent. Think here, for instance, of the stereotypes of "hysterical" or "oversensitive" women, "angry" Black men/women, the "melodramatic" gay, the "man-hating" lesbian.

In these ways, oppressive social structures can play an important—in some cases, crucial—role as tools of gaslighting. But, again, it is not the social structures themselves (e.g., the oppressive social norms or stereotypes), nor even their psychological internalization, that cause the gaslighting. Gaslighting is the work of *people* who use those already antecedently terrible aspects of the social structures as means of radically undermining their targets in ways that suit the aims of gaslighting.

4. The Tools of Gaslighting and Its Aims—The Right Tools for a Rotten Job

What do the eight central tools of gaslighters that I've mentioned in this chapter—trust, human sociability (and its dangerous counterpart, isolation), working presumptions of deliberative fallibility, love, empathy, practical considerations, authority and purported authority, and oppressive tropes and stereotypes—all have in common? They are all fundamental ways of organizing and orienting ourselves—our minds, our cares and concerns, our affects, our deliberations, and our self-conceptions—in relation to others and to the world. And all but the last of these involve questions that are not only fundamental but also unavoidable for all of us. Whom we trust, love, or empathize with in what ways and under what circumstances, with whom we have what kind of contact, how and when the deliberatively and conversationally necessary working hypothesis "I might be wrong" should be applied in a way that leads to active doubt, sorting out the likely practical consequences of our conduct and making appropriately prudential and moral decisions in part in that light, and figuring out when and in what ways claimed authority is legitimate—no one can avoid these questions.

There is, in this light, a horrifyingly good fit between the tools gaslighters use and their aims. Gaslighters seek to radically undermine their targets' fundamental deliberative and moral abilities—to the point that the targets no longer have standing as deliberators and moral agents. And to do that, they make perverse use of the very dispositions that are foundational to our deliberating and relating to others.

5

Social Structures, Subjugation, and Gaslighting

There's a better life and you dream about it don't you
It's a rich man's game, no matter what they call it
And you spend your life putting money in his wallet
(...) It's enough to drive you crazy if you let it

—DOLLY PARTON, *9 TO 5*

DOLLY PARTON'S famous song refers to phenomena that are all too familiar. Pernicious social structures—whether we're talking about the relatively small-scale structures of a particular organization or broader social structures like classism, racism, and sexism—can indeed be maddening. But should we call these *gaslighting* phenomena, perhaps under the rubric of a subcategory—"structural gaslighting"? There's been some movement in that direction in the past few years, both in the academic literature and in the popular press. In this chapter, I want to push back against these trends. My fundamental reasons for doing so are, in one respect, simple. If we extend our conception of gaslighting in the ways we'd need to in order to cover these cases, we'll lose sight of not only what's distinctive (interpersonally and morally) about the phenomenon for the sake of which the term was coined in the first place but also what's distinctive (interpersonally, morally, and politically) about the phenomena we are thereby absorbing under the title of gaslighting. On the other hand, if we reserve the term "gaslighting" for the interpersonal cases identified as our core phenomenon in chapters 1 to 4, then the *analogies and disanalogies* between gaslighting and these other structural and political phenomena become mutually illuminating, in much the way that learning about one family member can illuminate one's understanding of another.

1. What Is Structural Gaslighting?

Although the phrase "structural gaslighting" is increasingly common, it's applied in practice to a number of distinct phenomena. Sometimes what gets called "structural gaslighting" is the *use* of one or more aspects of a form of systematic subjugation—say a trope or stereotype like "women are empathetic" or "Black men are dangerous"—by a particular individual or set of individuals, as part of an effort to undermine another individual in ways that are recognizable as gaslighting. Certain aspects of pernicious social structures, in other words, can be used as tools by gaslighters. Moreover, they can be used by gaslighters in response to the target's protest against discriminatory conduct.[1] These are indeed two significant ways in which pernicious, especially discriminatory, social structures can play important roles in familiar cases of gaslighting. I myself highlighted both of these phenomena as features of gaslighting in my 2014 article and have discussed them more extensively here (in chapters 2 and 4). But calling these cases of "structural gaslighting" is misleading. To begin with, in these cases it's *not* the social structures that are doing the gaslighting. The gaslighting that's at issue in these cases is an undertaking of *a person or persons*. It's also morally misleading: precisely because in these cases we are talking about the conduct of persons, referring to these cases as instances of "structural gaslighting" conceals the fact that individual people are here the proper loci of moral responsibility.

Sometimes, on the other hand, the phrase "structural gaslighting" is used to refer to the thought that social structures themselves can "do the gaslighting." What this amounts to, unfortunately, can be less than clear. Sometimes the phrase is used extremely broadly to refer to any social structure that can have—in some metaphorical sense or another—"crazy making effects." But surely we don't want to describe *any* social structures that meet *that* characterization as aspects of "structural *gaslighting*." Completely anodyne social structures can have serious destabilizing effects on particular persons for reasons that speak to difficulties (psychological and/or moral) with those particular persons. People, for instance, who are accustomed to getting away with doing whatever they want

1. See, e.g., Crawford-Roberts et al., 2020; Davis and Earnst (2017).

can find their sense of themselves as deliberators and agents radically disrupted in ways that make them question their sanity, when / insofar as they are placed within organizational or social structures in which just rules are enforced fairly. We might even, if we are very careful with what we mean in saying it, say something like, "It's the organizational structure that's driving her crazy this way." But the *problem* in case like that is not that organizational structure—it's her. The organizational or social structure is treating her as an equally accountable agent, and her sense of herself is being radically disrupted precisely because she's unaccustomed to being held accountable.

For similar reasons, it won't be enough to amend the initial definition to say that structural gaslighting occurs when a social structure *tends* to make people question their sanity or makes a substantial group of people question their sanity. After all, in the same way that individuals who are accustomed to getting their way can be unmoored by finding themselves in organizational structures that treat them as accountable equals, so too groups of people who are accustomed to having unjust forms of social power and unearned advantages not infrequently feel unmoored when required to live under more just social arrangements. They haven't been gaslit.

Should we deal with this by adding a substantive clause, namely, "structural gaslighting" occurs only when it is both the case that a social structure tends to leave a substantial group of people questioning their sanity *and* that social structure is politically or morally pernicious? Even that seems vague and overbroad—in want of more specificity as to what ought to qualify as both the "right" kind of political or moral perniciousness and the "right" kind of questioning one's sanity for a case to qualify as "structural gaslighting."

In the past few years a particular way of giving greater precision to this latter kind of usage of "structural gaslighting"—where it's the structures themselves that are seen as "doing" the gaslighting—has emerged as increasingly standard in the philosophical literature. Here, for instance, is one fairly well-known characterization of structural gaslighting: "Structural gaslighting describes any conceptual work that functions to obscure the nonaccidental connections between structures of oppression and the patterns of harm that they produce and license."[2] I take it that the basic idea is this. A social structure is of the relevant sort to play a role in "structural gaslighting" when it is, or is part of, some system of subjugation—racism, sexism, classism, and so on. Such structures, the thought goes, are aptly described as "gaslighting" insofar as it is in the nature of those structures that, in some way or another, they obscure the very fact *that* they are subjugating structures. For instance, as several of the articles on this topic point out, it is not a coincidence that the conceptual lacunae Fricker calls "hermeneutical injustices" occur where they do—in arenas that involve aspects of the experience of subjugation.[3] And it is certainly plausible to suppose, as do these authors, that such lacunae play an important role in maintaining the relevant systems of subjugation. To use Fricker's own central example of a hermeneutical injustice—it's awfully difficult to fight sexual harassment if you lack that phrase and everyone around you keeps interpreting events as

2. Berenstain, 2020. See also Bailey, 2020.

3. See, for instance, the articles in the volume of *Hypatia* (35, no. 4, 2020) devoted to "Gaslighting and Epistemic Injustice," especially Berenstain, 2020. Fricker defines hermeneutical injustice as occurring whenever "someone has a significant area of their social experience obscured from understanding owing to prejudicial flaws in shared resources for social interpretation" (2007, chap. 7, abstract).

"harmless flirting." The insistence on reading those interactions as "harmless flirting" is not just mistaken—it's mistaken in a way that conceals the sexist harm of, and sexism involved in, what is in fact sexual harassment.

Hermeneutical injustice is only one example of a dimension of systems of subjugation that works this way. Indeed, virtually *every* dimension of sexism, racism, classism, and so on has what we might call a "self-disguising" feature. Even something as simple as the sexist or racist norms like "women shouldn't be bartenders" and "Black people and white people should drink from separate fountains" works in part by being disguised for the oppressive norms that they are. Sometimes the disguise is as simple as the coding of an oppressive norm as something other than oppressive—as when it is part of the gender norm itself that it's imagined to be appropriate based on alleged sex differences.[4] Sometimes it's a bit more complicated. For instance, one way that sexist norms get disguised for what they are is in being presented as purportedly descriptive claims: so "women should be especially empathetic" gets coded as the purportedly descriptive claim "women are especially empathetic," encouraging women to feel defective qua women insofar as they fail to meet what they imagine to be the standard for qualifying thereby as a woman, triggering

---

4. Think, for instance, of the ways in which sexist laws prohibiting women from certain kinds of work were widely held to be justified on the basis of purported sex differences. When Michigan banned women from being bartenders, *not a single justice* thought there was anything inappropriate, much less illegal, about it. In the words of the court, there was nothing "irrational" about banning women from being bartenders. The only dispute in the court was whether there was an invidious discrimination if *some women* (the wives and daughters of bar owners) were allowed to be bartenders, while other women were not. *Goesaert v. Cleary*, 335 U.S. 464 (1948).

stereotype threat and so on.[5] In being "self-disguising" in such ways as these, racist and sexist social structures are no different from racist and sexist people: they're not going to stand up and tell you they're racist and sexist but will instead do everything possible to disguise that fact. It's not surprising then that those who hold that "structural gaslighting" is at issue whenever there's an oppressive social structure that's self-disguising also see that phrase as widely applicable—they see it as implicated in every dimension of oppressive social structures like racism and sexism that have a "self-disguising" feature, and virtually every dimension of oppressive social structures has such a "self-disguising feature."

I think this is a mistake, and I think once we see why, we'll be able to see there's good reason to simply steer clear of the phrase "structural gaslighting." In fact, I think that recognizing the particular ways in which the self-disguising features of particular dimensions of subjugating systems are politically and morally pernicious gives us very strong reason to conceptualize them as something other than gaslighting.

2. Some Oppressive Social Structures and Their Similarities to Gaslighting

It's easiest to gain clarity about this by first thinking in a bit more detail about a few particular dimensions of subjugating systems that have the kind of self-disguising feature that advocates of the phrase "structural gaslighting" seem to have in mind. I'll take, as my central example, the "double bind," though I'll also have a

---

5. Fine, 2010, discusses this aspect of this particular sexist trope at length.

bit to say in this context about hermeneutical injustices (because those have been highlighted by advocates for broadening our conception of gaslighting to include "structural gaslighting") and ordinary prejudicial norms and stereotypes.

Let's start then with the double bind. At the most basic level, a double bind is any set of "irreconcilable demands or a choice between two [or more] undesirable options."[6] In the context of oppressive systems, the demands and/or choices themselves are the product of that system (e.g., sexism or racism). So, for example, women today often face what's called the "competence dilemma." A woman can choose forms of self-presentation that emphasize her competence, but then she'll be seen as unlikeable. Or she can choose forms of self-presentation that make her seem likeable, but then she'll be seen as incompetent. Either way she'll be seen as a less desirable hire than men who, not facing this choice, have the option to appear both likeable and competent.[7] One of the most bitingly accurate representations of sexist workplace double binds that I've seen appeared in the online humor magazine *McSweeney's*. Headlined "Reasons You Were Not Promoted That Are Totally Unrelated to Gender," it reads in part,

- You don't smile enough. People don't like you.
- You smile too much. People don't take you seriously.

6. This is the definition that appears in the Google search engine's "Dictionary Box" when one types "double bind" into the search engine. Google attributes the definition to Oxford Languages. The *Cambridge Dictionary*, 2023, similarly provides as a definition, "a difficult situation in which, whatever action you decide to take, you cannot escape unpleasant results."

7. See, e.g., Litwin, 2020.

- You're abrasive. For example, that time when you asked for a raise. It was awkward and you made the men on the senior leadership team uncomfortable.
- You don't speak up. We'd really like to see you take on more of a leadership role before we pay you for being a leader.
- You're sloppy. Like when you sent that email with a typo. You need to proofread your work.
- You're too focused on details. Leaders need to take the 50,000-foot fighter pilot view. No, I never served in the armed forces. What's your point?[8]

Double binds like these—those that are the outgrowth of systems of subjugation—present choice conditions under which there are no good options *because* that's how sexist, racist, or other oppressive norms so configure the situation. One clear sense in which there's no good option is that there's no option on which one is, say, as promotable as a man. But as Sukaina Hirji argues, at a deeper cut, when there are oppressive social structures in play, one's choices can be such that every option is one in which one will end up contributing to one's own oppression.[9] Take, for instance, the first bullet point in the *McSweeney's* bit. The sexist norm at issue here is something like "women must smile a lot to be seen as likeable." A woman who resists this sexist norm pays the (prudential) price of being seen as unlikeable, and insofar as she's seen as unlikeable, this also thereby reduces her ability to engage in the forms of social

8. Mojtabai, 2015.
9. Hirji, 2021.

cooperation that make it possible to fight oppression. But the woman who acquiesces and smiles is not much better off—sure, she gets to be seen as likeable, but insofar as her acquiescing to the sexist norm helps reinforce it, and thereby reinforce sexist norms more generally, she too engages in conduct that runs counter to her own objective interests. In part in light of such considerations, Hirji argues that we should see the defining characteristic of the oppressive double bind this way: "Because of the way an agent's own prudential good is bound up with their ability to resist oppression, double binds are choice situations where no matter what an agent does, they become a mechanism in their own oppression." Or, put slightly differently, these are "choice situations where an agent is forced to choose between either cooperating with or resisting some oppressive norm, and in which whatever they do, they end up reinforcing to some degree the oppressive structures that constrain their options."[10]

The fact that one's choices are configured and constrained in this way is true whether or not one recognizes that one's choice situation constitutes an oppressive double bind. That's a feature of the relevant social norms. But some of the *power* of double binds, both in terms of some of their ill effects and in terms of the role they play in reinforcing subjugating norms, derives partly from ways in which they tend to be self-disguising. It can be very difficult to recognize that one is in a double bind, rather than, say, facing a simple choice between resisting a sexist demand ("be more likeable!") and acting prudently by conforming to the oppressive norm. And even when one

10. Hirji, 2021, 645, 658.

does recognize *that* one is in a double bind, it can be extremely tempting to think that there's a way out—one that would at least be "the most prudent" or the option that would contribute least to one's own oppression. Moreover, to the extent one is caught in that trap (a trap encouraged by the very oppressive structures that create the double bind in the first place), it is hard to resist the temptation to inappropriately blame or criticize oneself or others for choices made under conditions of a double bind, and for thereby contributing to our own or their own oppression.[11]

Oppressive double binds thus fit the characterization of "structural gaslighting" that's becoming standard: it's a dimension of discriminatory/subjugating systems that has self-disguising features on account of which it partly derives its power (in terms of the role that it plays in those systems of subjugation). There are also particular aspects of the *way* that double binds work that bear close similarities to the way in which interpersonal gaslighting works. They both present as situations that are, in some sense, *escapable*. If only one could find the right thing to say to the gaslighter, or "better" evidence, or more, or be "less emotional" in presenting the evidence, then (one thinks) maybe then the gaslighter will see. . . . In the double bind, similarly, it's all too easy to think that if one did smile more (or less), then even if the demand to smile more (or less) is sexist, doing so will somehow release one from the social penalty of violating that sexist norm, and somehow get that benefit without simultaneously reinforcing the sexist norm. Moreover, in both cases, the appearance of escapability is one

11. See esp. Hirji, 2021, 668.

of the ways in which one's agency is turned against oneself, making one complicit in one's own oppression and/or psychological undoing (in the case of gaslighting).

There are also parallels between the way in which situations of hermeneutical injustice do the kind of damage they do and the ways that interpersonal gaslighting works. For instance, in both cases the difficulty involved in pointing to the problem is baked into the structure of the situation. In the case of interpersonal gaslighting, one of the many such difficulties (as we've seen) is that the ability to point to the problem necessarily involves pointing to a *pattern*. Even more seriously, as we saw in chapter 4, gaslighting works in part because gaslighters make pernicious use of what are otherwise good deliberative and conversational norms—like the norm that one should approach just about any given situation recognizing that one might be wrong—in ways that are extremely difficult to recognize in situ as the perversion of those norms that's at issue when one is being gaslit. In cases of hermeneutical injustices, the relevant difficulty is that which is borne of the very conceptual lacunae that define the hermeneutical injustice—it's awfully difficult to point to a problem for which one literally has no name.

We can even point to a similar such self-disguising aspect of many ordinary prejudicial norms and stereotypes. In fact, we've already seen as much in section 1. Many such subjugating norms come disguised as descriptive claims like "women are more empathetic than men" or "women are less argumentative than men." Buried within such purportedly descriptive claims are sexist normative expectations, such that to fail to be more empathetic than (some imagined set of) men, or less argumentative, is to fail to meet a normative standard of womanhood. That's why gender priming has the effects that it does.[12]

3. Why Not Structural Gaslighting?

And yet, I want to urge that we not broaden our conception of gaslighting to include such social-structural issues under a new subcategory of "structural gaslighting." All of the various social structures that we've seen here fit common characterizations of the kind of social structure that's supposed to be implicated in "structural gaslighting" are in fact very different from one another. And they differ from one another in ways that go to the heart of our reasons for coining different names for these different phenomena. They differ in their defining harms (the harms that are inextricable from the existence of the phenomena in question), the other kinds of damage they typically inflict, the central loci of responsibility for those harms, and the means by which those harms are caused. These are significant aspects of everyday social life, and we need language that allows us to name and point to the social phenomena that are constituted by these widely variant features. If we group all of them under the heading of "gaslighting" we risk losing our ability to recognize, point to, and name the very distinct phenomena that are picked out by these concepts. The term "gaslighting," for instance, would lose not only its association with forms of *interpersonal* interaction but also its association with the very distinctive ways of being radically

12. See Fine, 2010, for an extensive discussion of the relationship among the such purportedly descriptive claims, their normative import, and gender priming.

undermined that get captured in colloquial definitions as "questioning one's own sanity" and "being driven crazy." The same is true on the other side(s) of the coin—there are distinctive harms involved in hermeneutical injustices, double binds, and run-of-the-mill oppressive social norms, and we'll lose the ability to point to those distinctive harms to the extent that we amalgamate them all under the title of "structural gaslighting." Finally, given that there are very different harms involved in each, it would be *morally* misleading to regard them under the single heading of "gaslighting."

A. Defining (or Constitutive) Harms, Loci of Responsibility, Means by Which Harms Occur

All of these reasons to avoid talk of "structural gaslighting" turn on the same basic thought—we're talking here about different social phenomena, and to speak of them all as engaged in "gaslighting" (whether "structural" or not) obscures those essential differences. So let's think about those differences, starting with their defining harms. Interpersonal gaslighting and the oppressive social structures we've been talking about harm in various ways, some of which are situationally dependent. But *some* of the harms, in each case, are inextricably intertwined with the very existence of the phenomenon at issue, and it is those harms to which I am here referring as "defining harms." In gaslighting, the defining harms involve the target's being radically undermined as deliberator and agent, and having a *sense of herself* as having been incapacitated (to some extent) as deliberator and moral agent. In the more colloquial terms with which we began in chapter 1, the defining harms of gaslighting are having one's sanity seriously undermined and commensurately questioning one's sanity. These harms are part of any recognizable definition of gaslighting. The defining harms of double binds, hermeneutical injustices, and social tropes/stereotypes are very different. Oppressive double binds, as such, put agents in situations in which they cannot but be complicit in their own oppression.[13] Hermeneutical injustices, as such, harm insofar as the conceptual lacunae in which they consist mean members of oppressed groups lack the resources to articulate or understand some aspect of their experience as members of that group.[14] Oppressive social norms, like "women should be (more) empathetic (than men)" and "women should raise children and not be employed," harm by creating unjust expectations for members of the target group.

Not only are each of these very different sorts of harms, but there's a particular kind of chasm between the harms that are inextricable from the phenomenon of gaslighting on the one hand, and on the other the harms constitutively tied to the various features of oppressive social structures mentioned. The harms that are constitutively tied to gaslighting must be specified in terms of states of the agent—she questions her sanity, her deliberative and agential capacities are radically undermined, she loses standing as deliberator and agent on account of the ways in which her capacities are undermined, and so on. In contrast, harms constitutively associated with the various social structures we've been talking about are harms that are specifiable without reference to anything about the agent's psychology.

13. Hirji, 2021.
14. Fricker, 2007.

Or, to put it slightly differently, I don't need to know one single thing about what is going on in the mind of someone who is a member of a relevantly subjugated group to know whether or not they have been harmed (in at least some ways) by the double binds, hermeneutical injustices, and oppressive social norms that are applicable to members of that group.

The phenomena in question also differ fundamentally in terms of the primary loci of moral responsibility—in gaslighting, the primary locus of responsibility is the person or persons doing the gaslighting. In the case of double binds, hermeneutical injustices, and oppressive social norms, there's often no particular person(s) on whom responsibility for the harms rest (this is, of course, the one difference implicitly acknowledged by those who use the phrase "structural gaslighting").[15] The means by which a person is successfully gaslit also differ enormously from the ways in which (or means by which) people are brought to experience double binds, hermeneutical injustices, stereotypes. To the extent that social structures are the cause of the harms at issue in the latter set of cases, no *person* need do anything in order for the harms in question to occur—let alone engage in the kinds of grotesque manipulations over extended periods of time that are characteristic means of gaslighting.

In all of these ways, gaslighting is a fundamentally very different phenomenon from the features of oppressive social structures that some have suggested we see as "structural gaslighting." In

15. "Often" because individuals can deploy stereotypes and take advantage of the social structures that create hermeneutical injustices or double binds in ways that make those individuals morally responsible.

fact, seen in this light, it's not even clear why one would be *tempted* to adopt the term "gaslighting" as a way of characterizing either the nature of the harms these structures produce or how the structures work so as to produce those harms.

B. With Specific Regard to the "Self-Disguising" Aspects of Oppressive Social Structures

Perhaps, however, it will be suggested that I'm not looking in the right place. Advocates of the phrase "structural gaslighting" might point to the stress they've laid on the *self-disguising* aspects of oppressive social structures. Yet a close look will show us that even focusing on those features of the oppressive social structures at issue won't bring us close enough to something recognizable as gaslighting to warrant that name. If it's the self-disguising features of those social structures that gives us reason to group them together under the rubric of "structural gaslighting," then it has to be something about the way the self-disguising features of those social structures *work* that makes it look like a case of gaslighting.[16] And for that to be the case, there should at least be something about what (typically) happens to a person caught in one of these pernicious

16. It can't be the mere fact that these social structures have self-disguising dimensions that gives us warrant for saying they're aspects of "structural gaslighting." To see this, think about the parallel with some strictly interpersonal cases. All kinds of bad actors rely to some extent on disguising what they're up to in order to get away with it. Not only the liar but also the thief, the conman, and the woman who puts on a "damsel in distress" act to gain attention all disguise their true intentions in order to get away with their designs. That doesn't make their conduct qualify as "gaslighting," and we're not tempted to think otherwise.

structures—something that happens to that person in virtue of their not recognizing the oppressive social structure for what it is—that puts them in roughly the same agent-state as that in which someone who has been successfully gaslit finds herself.

There's no mystery at this point about in what agent-state the person who has been gaslit finds herself. Successful gaslighting leaves its target gravely undermined as deliberator and agent—being gaslit seriously damages her abilities to form relevant justified beliefs, to reasonably assess her situation, to protest wrongdoing, to morally deliberate, and so on. As we've seen repeatedly and in a variety of ways, there's a world of difference between being uncertain what to believe about some particular matter and doubting one's capacity to form apt beliefs, a vast chasm of difference between being manipulated into believing a lie and being manipulated into questioning one's basic deliberative abilities, between having the evidence that allows one to form apt beliefs concealed from one's view and having one's capacities to form apt beliefs undermined. These are differences we need to bear in mind when comparing the state of the successfully gaslit person to the state(s) in which people caught in oppressive social structures who don't recognize that fact find themselves.

In this light, consider what it looks like when someone faces a double bind, or a situation of hermeneutical injustice, or an oppressive social norm, and the self-disguising aspects of those structures fully obscure the very fact that the person is in such a situation. The person who does not recognize that she's in an oppressive double bind will falsely believe she has a choice between a prudential option (e.g., smiling to appear likable), and an option in which she resists oppressive structures (refusing to smile and thereby resisting the sexist norm). As Hirji points out, this in turn will makes one (wrongly) appear criticizable for making a choice in which one is complicit in one's own oppression.[17,18] Experiencing misplaced criticism of this sort (from others or from oneself) can be a serious matter, but it's very different from being induced to question one's sanity—one's basic abilities as deliberator and moral agent—or having those basic abilities seriously undermined. And it's quite doubtful that a case could even be made that the function of the kind of misplaced criticisms that are frequent sequelae to disguised double binds is to make the agent question her basic deliberative abilities. To begin with, I'm *more* likely to see myself as appropriately subject to the kinds of criticism that are at issue here if I'm confident in my deliberative abilities. Second, the misplaced criticisms that come into play when one doesn't see that one is in an oppressive double bind—in stark contrast to the criticisms involved in gaslighting—don't target one's basic deliberative abilities. The core misplaced criticism in the case of double binds is either, depending on what choice one makes, that one has acted prudentially at the cost of reifying subjugating social structures, or that one resisted oppressive social structures where one ought to have acted prudentially.

17. One might still be criticizable in other ways—e.g., for not doing what one can to ameliorate the oppression-reifying effects of one's choices or for refusing to acknowledge the ways in which one's choices in line with (sexist, racist, etc.) expectations are socially rewarded.

18. Hirji, 2021, 668.

A person who does not recognize that her situation is one of hermeneutical injustice—that is, a situation where there aren't the conceptual resources to describe some aspect of her experiences as a member of oppressed group—will certainly struggle in ways that are specifically the result of her not seeing her situation for what it is. She may continue to think there's something objectionable about her experience and struggle with the frustration and exhaustion of trying to explain what's objectionable about her experience to others and herself, perhaps criticizing herself for not being able to come up with the right words, not realizing that the words just aren't there. Or in the face of such ongoing frustration, she might just give up and decide that the problem was her all along, concluding for instance that it really was "just harmless flirting" and she was mistaken to be upset about it. Either way, the person in a situation of hermeneutical injustice she doesn't see as such is harmed precisely because she can't see the situation for what it is—but she's not left in the same kind of state as is the person who has been successfully gaslit.

What about the person who doesn't recognize that what she's dealing with is an oppressive social norm? One common result is an adaptive preference—the complete internalization of the oppressive norm; a woman's preference for shaved legs, or the desire to be saved by or led by a man, for instance.[19] Of course, the prevalence of oppressive norms and their widespread social enforcement is such that one can end up with an adaptive preference—most of us have some of them—even

19. On the relationship between adaptive preferences and double binds, see Hirji 2021, 668.

if one sees those oppressive social norms for what they are. But one is much more likely to develop and maintain such adaptive preferences if one doesn't see that the norm to which one is adapting oneself is oppressive. Moreover, if one does not see the norm in question as oppressive, then one absolutely cannot see *that* one's preference is adaptive, or even so much as entertain that possibility, let alone act appropriately in response to that knowledge. On the other hand, suppose that, while failing to see that what one is dealing with is an oppressive social norm, one doesn't develop an adaptive preference. What then? Well, if you don't see that a social norm is an oppressive one, or perhaps don't even quite clearly see that it is a *norm* rather than a description of, say, "how women are," then you'll evaluate whatever happen to be your desires, preferences, and choices (wrongly) as either defective in virtue of falling short of it or (equally mistakenly) as especially laudatory on account of your conformity to it.[20] And you'll similarly so evaluate others subject to the norm. That can be an awful experience, but it's not remotely the same experience as being radically undermined as deliberator and moral agent.

Such are the results when the self-disguising features of double binds, hermeneutical injustices, and oppressive social norms successfully hide from view the nature of these dimensions of oppressive social structures. They're terrible—from the adaptive preference not recognized as such, to the frustration

---

20. Understanding this is important for understanding a number of related phenomena, like gender priming. For instance, when primed with the stereotype that women morally reason with greater focus on "care-based" considerations, women adduced more care-based considerations in debating a hypothetical. Fine, 2010, 25.

and exhaustion involved in ongoing attempts to articulate that for which there are no words, to unwarranted shame and guilt that results from unwarranted criticism. But these terrible effects are deeply different from the results of successful gaslighting. And the point isn't just that calling what these social structures do to those who fall under their purview "gaslighting" obscures what's distinctively awful about gaslighting (though it does, and that's important). It also obscures what's distinctively awful about each of these structural phenomena— double binds, hermeneutical injustices, oppressive social norms. That's equally important. Our language should mark these differences.

C. What Dolly Parton Sees

Still, there's something in the vicinity of all of this—neither quite gaslighting, nor the sort of structural phenomena we've been talking about—that we haven't yet discussed, and that I suspect lies behind at least some of the temptation to use the phrase "structural gaslighting." It's the kind of phenomena about which Dolly Parton is singing in "9 to 5." Those phenomena can't be made to fit the definition of "structural gaslighting" discussed in section 2. Dolly Parton isn't singing about something she doesn't recognize for what it is. She understands perfectly well that she's up against something unfair and systemic ("it's a rich man's game, no matter what they call it") against which she cannot win through individual effort. She has no difficulty naming it. Neither, however, do the phenomena about which she sings sit easily under the rubric of interpersonal gaslighting. Although the story of "9 to 5" is narrated first-personally, the author isn't confused, or doubting herself, or mistrustful of her ability to think through her situation or decide what to do. She is perfectly clear-eyed about all of this. And yet, for all that, she is also expressing first-personally another sentiment that's deeply true: "it's enough to drive you crazy if you let it."

Here's the sort of situation that we can be pretty sure that Dolly Parton has in mind—it's the plotline of the movie to which "9 to 5" is the title song.[21] The boss is sexist in every possible way. He tells one woman employee to go buy a scarf for his wife, under threat of not supporting the promotion she's been seeking ("be a team player!"). When she gets the scarf, he gives it to a secretary, whom he literally chases around the desk and tries to grab and kiss (not for the first time). He tells all the other women employees falsely that he's actually sleeping with the secretary, the result of which is that they're hostile to her and she's isolated without path for complaint even to coworkers. When the scarf-buying woman comes back to his office with an idea for streamlining office work, he tells her the idea is flawed, but turns around and passes it up the food chain and takes credit for it; when she calls him out on it, he threatens her job. And for good measure, he fires some women whom his minion overhears in the bathroom comparing salaries, thereby ensuring that all the other women in the company know he's serious about such threats. At the same time, the business is organized so that effective complaint about any of this impossible—for example, there are few channels for complaint, and those that exist are set up so that the complaint will

21. What follows are narrative snippets from the movie *9 to 5* (1980).

go nowhere. Stuck in the system, financially dependent on the job, the women spend their days dealing with discrimination and harassment, making impossible unjust choices (buying the scarf, rebuffing advances, deciding whether to call him out for stealing ideas) all the while knowing that there is no choice that will allow them to escape the injustice. To call this aggravating would be a vast understatement. As Lily Tomlin's character in the movie—*Violet*—says when her coworker Betty advises "don't let him get to you," "You're right, I tell myself the same thing, but Betty inside I can feel the pressure building up. I can't take much more of this, something sometime is going to snap and then. . . ."

What we're imagining, in short, is dealing with ongoing bigotry and discrimination in the context of a corrupt system (whether that system is a company or an entire social system). The relevant forms of corruption here include not only that the system itself is discriminatory but also that no matter what one does, there will be no accountability and no remedy for the discriminatory conduct of individuals within the system. This leads entirely reasonably to tremendous levels of anger, aggravation, resentment, and indignation. But precisely because there's no possibility of remedy or accountability, there is no way for those reactive attitudes to be expressed such that they will have even minimally adequate uptake. It doesn't take clinical experience or research studies to know that that's untenable—as Violet points out, the pressure of such contained anger builds over time, and it eventually has to go somewhere. And the more that's true, the more its eventual expression is going to be such as is perceived as unreasonable. Unhinged. Overreaction. Oversensitive. Acting out. Crazed.

In whatever way the anger ends up expressed (even if it's not in kidnapping your sexist boss), it's apt to be interpreted under some such description for three reasons. First, it will be the expression of anger long suppressed (for the sake of prudence if nothing else, of the sort required to keep one's job), so it's likely to be a very strong expression of anger. Second, the true object of anger in such cases is not whatever ends up being the immediate precipitating incident (the last straw) but the whole string or pattern of events. But that is a fact that can elude onlookers, making the anger seem disproportionate in ways that it's not. Third, remember that all this is occurring in the context of a discriminatory/oppressive system. One aspect of every such system is tropes about members of marginalized groups that portray them as emotionally dysregulated, especially with regard to negative emotions: the hysterical woman, the angry Black man, the angry Black woman, and so on. The social availability of such tropes incentivizes interpretations of members of those groups that fit the trope, both in general and especially in situations like these where strong negative emotions are being expressed. Being thus interpreted as hysterical, unreasonable, overreacting, or acting out is likely to only intensify the anger at the original pattern of incidents. And so on.

Betty's advice, "don't let him get to you," is about the best one can do in circumstances like these, but it's advice with serious limitations. For one, preserving enough self-respect (in the colloquial sense) not to be actively self-undermining requires acknowledging ongoing bad conduct for what it is, and that comes hand in hand with anger, indignation, resentment. Similarly, to the extent that the advice amounts to "focus on something else," in circumstances like these that's not only psychologically difficult advice but also advice one can follow only to a limited extent: the context is one of ongoing bigotry and discrimination, and prudentially, one has to deal with that.

The song "9 to 5" captures both sides of this coin: the sense in which engaging with systems like this will "drive you crazy," the inevitability of that, and the nevertheless sage advice to limit the damage and anger as best one can by limiting one's engagement with the discriminatory system and the bigoted individuals within it. The role of systemic matters is unmistakable. And the analogies with gaslighting aren't hard to spot: the accusations of overreacting, acting out, and being unhinged in response to protests against bad conduct and/or corrupt systems, the fact that an adequate understanding of such situations requires that one see individual incidents in the context of patterns over time, the fact that all of this puts the target in a terrible position emotionally, and a position in which focusing on anything other than this set of interactions will be psychologically difficult and often prudentially ill-advised.

But it's not gaslighting. The disanalogies are as apparent as the analogies. And there are moral and political reasons to emphasize the disanalogies. One way to see the moral difference brings us back to where we began at the beginning of this section: the person in the position of which Dolly Parton speaks is perfectly sane, perfectly clear-eyed. And she *feels* sane in the sense relevant to gaslighting—perfectly capable of deliberating well, self-assured in her moral assessment of the situation. When Parton sings "it's enough to drive you crazy if you let it," she's not using "crazy" to refer to the feelings of being

unmoored that are characteristic of the successfully gaslit—
the emotional state that Hepburn's character in *Pat and Mike*
captures by describing herself as feeling "carved up, nobody";
the state Beauvoir captures by saying, "I am no longer sure
what I think, or even if I think at all." Instead, Dolly Parton is
using "crazy" as a metaphor for both the extreme feelings of
frustration, anger, futility that are natural sequelae of being
trapped in the kind of discriminatory environment with which
we meet in "9 to 5," and the meta-level feelings of frustration,
anger, and futility one feels when, in virtue of being trapped
in such a discriminatory environment, one has no avenue by
which to safely express those first-order feelings of frustration,
anger, and futility. Moreover, the aim of "the system" of "9 to 5"
(and the bosses who enforce it) isn't to radically undermine
the subjugated as deliberators and moral agents—it's to use
their abilities to reinforce the system itself. As Dolly Parton
says, "You spend your life putting money in his wallet," and
she knows as well as we that that's how the system is *supposed*
to work.

4. The Big Picture

It's worth reminding ourselves what rejection of the notion of
"structural gaslighting" amounts to in this context. "Structural
gaslighting" is supposed to be a structural counterpart of the
interpersonal phenomenon. The interpersonal phenomenon of
gaslighting, we've seen, involves a characteristic configuration
of aims, motives, means by which those aims are accomplished,
and harms (in the broad sense). These characteristic aims, motives, methods, means, and harms not only are recognizable

features of interpersonal gaslighting but also make gaslighting recognizably *different* from lying, brainwashing, guilt-tripping, shaming, and so forth. For the phrase "structural gaslighting" to be apt, it would need to make sense to attribute to a particular set of social structures a structural analogue to the configuration of aims, motives, methods, means, and harms that characterize interpersonal gaslighting. With that in mind, we've examined a variety of social structures sometimes thought to be instances of "structural gaslighting" and seen that none are aptly so labeled. It's *possible* that there exists some social structure that's relevantly analogous enough to interpersonal gaslighting to make appropriate the label "structural gaslighting." The kind of argument in which I've been here engaged isn't the sort that could exclude, in advance of examining the details, that possibility. But given that none of the most plausible candidates for "structural gaslighting" are aptly so labeled, healthy skepticism about future invocations of that phrase is warranted.

There are many rotten things in social life; many of these make life substantially worse for members of marginalized communities—directly or indirectly. They are not all the same bad things, and we do ourselves no favors if we reconstruct the conceptual world in ways that elide the distinctions among these various pernicious social phenomena.

6

The Multidimensional Moral Horror Show of Gaslighting

AS TEMPTING as it might be to suppose otherwise, there is no simple, univocal answer to the question "what's wrong with gaslighting?" Gaslighting is unethical along various dimensions and involves many different kinds of wrongdoing. The central aim of this chapter is to elucidate each of these wrongs, to do so in a way that shows that there is no central or primary way in which gaslighting is wrong, and to make a case thereby that part of what makes gaslighting so awful is the very fact of its multidimensional immorality.

We'll begin in section 1 by thinking about gaslighting as a species of manipulation, asking whether common views about what's wrong with manipulating someone might illuminate the wrongs of gaslighting and, if so, in what way. Section 2 considers the epistemic wrongs of gaslighting, and section 3 is concerned with wrongs that have to do specifically with the tools that gaslighters use in their efforts to undo their targets. In section 4 I consider the wrongs involved in the fact that targets of gaslighting are made complicit in their own undoing. This is followed in section 5 by an examination of gaslighting as a form of "silencing." Section 6 discusses the psychological harms of gaslighting, focusing on depression. Getting the phenomenon of gaslighting in view requires getting this entire panoply of wrongs properly into view.

1. Gaslighting as a Form of Manipulation

One might imagine that the question of what's wrong with gaslighting has a simple and straightforward answer. As one author puts in, given that gaslighting is a form of manipulation, "it follows that the wrong-making feature of manipulative gaslighting is whatever the wrong-making feature of wrongful manipulation is."[1] But that thought is seriously mistaken, and even if it weren't mistaken it wouldn't be helpful. It's mistaken for two reasons. First, as we'll see later in this chapter, there are aspects of the wrongs of gaslighting that cannot be captured by focusing on the ways in which gaslighting is manipulative. Second, the territory covered by the term "manipulation" is too vast, and the peculiarities of gaslighting are too numerous and significant for it to be tenable to suppose that gaslighting and every other form of manipulation are wrong in the same ways and/or for the same reasons.[2] Furthermore, the question of

---

1. Stark, 2019, 233n10.

2. The distinction between the ways in which conduct is wrong and the reasons it is wrong is a subtle one that's only sometimes helpful insofar as our question is the first-order normative one of what's wrong with a certain form of conduct. In what follows, I mark the difference where it's relevant, but my primary focus is the question of what's wrong with gaslighting.

what's wrong with other (non-gaslighting) forms of manipulation, much less the question of what's wrong with manipulation per se, is very much under dispute. So even if we were to stipulate that whatever is wrong with manipulation is what's wrong with gaslighting, that would tell us very little.

All that said, it is certainly morally *relevant* that gaslighting belongs in the same general category with misconduct like guilt-trips, emotional blackmail, "playing the victim," and so on. Gaslighting is indeed a form of manipulation: it's one of any number of ways of interacting with people that involve morally problematic means of influence or control, means of influence that are not reducible to mere force or forced choice. The goal of this section is to figure out in precisely what ways that fact is morally relevant. We'll begin by taking close look at some of the ways in which the manipulation involved in gaslighting is idiosyncratic. In light of these idiosyncrasies, we'll then take up the issue of whether, and if so how, some of the common ways of understanding what's wrong with manipulation can help us pinpoint what's wrong with gaslighting in particular.

If we want to think about the ways in which the kind of manipulation that's involved in gaslighting is idiosyncratic, there's no better place to start than where this book began, with the things gaslighters say: "that's crazy," "don't be paranoid," "you're just acting out," "there's no pattern," "you're imagining things," and so on. In the context of gaslighting, such utterances are part of a pattern of conduct that's meant to work on targets in particular ways. Notice that the first three of these phrases involve colloquialisms that straddle evaluative realms. "Crazy," "paranoid," and "acting out" often function in everyday language as terms that are at once pseudo-medical and moral. That is, they are meant to communicate both that the person is not psychologically well and that there is something morally objectionable about her perspective, attitudes, or behavior. Such uses are not unique to the context of gaslighting. Consider, for instance, the ways in which the word "crazy" was/is often used in discourse about the Trump administration. Maureen Dowd once penned an op-ed column titled simply "Crazy Is as Crazy Does," the content of which is—as one would predict—a combination of morally outraged shock at a list of Trump's conduct and, on the other hand, various ways of expressing in newspaper-polite ease the psychological question, "What's wrong with this guy?"[3] Likewise with "paranoid" and its more recent cousin, "acting out"—both were originally terms having to do with specific ways of being/acting psychologically unwell, and both are now employed just as often to simultaneously convey moral condemnation. Claims like "there's no pattern" and "you're just imagining things" can be used in similar ways to *imply* that a person is both psychologically unwell and responding to a situation in a morally objectionable fashion.

When used in this double-edged way, such assertions create a fraught interpersonal situation—one that the gaslighter first introduces and then exploits. On the surface, what's fraught is that these phrases communicate a double whammy of both psychological and moral condemnation. But the situation in which this dual accusation places the target is more complex than that. Think about the stance we adopt toward someone when we think of her as seriously psychologically unwell. A central feature of this stance is the overwhelming

3. Dowd, 2019.

tendency to see those who are psychologically unwell as beyond the reach of reason and the condition with which they're afflicted as an excusing one, or at least potentially so.[4] We adopt what Strawson calls the "objective stance" toward them—we see them as an object of "treatment," someone to be "managed or handled or cured or trained." "If your attitude towards someone is wholly objective," Strawson writes, "then though you may fight with him, you cannot quarrel with him, and though you may talk with him, you cannot reason with him. You may at most pretend to quarrel, or to reason, with him."[5] Moral attitudes like anger, resentment, indignation, guilt, and shame, in contrast, are experienced from a standpoint in which we regard that person as a responsible participant in ethical life—one capable of reasoning her way to clearheaded views about what

4. I intend this as a description of the outlines of our operative concepts of mental health and illness. The details of how this works in practice and the ways in which it intersects with the stance we take when we speak of a person in *moral* terms are substantially more complicated than these outlines suggest. For example, believing someone is psychologically unwell often functions as an excusing condition in the manner suggested by this general outline. And it's in the nature of the judgment that someone is seriously psychologically unwell that the *possibility* is thereby raised that some of their conduct must be excused. But being psychologically unwell doesn't *always* excuse and certainly doesn't excuse everything. Such details are important for some purposes, but what is important here is the basic gestalt shift that is typically involved in shifting from seeing someone as psychologically unwell to evaluating her in moral terms. It's that gestalt shift that's important for understanding the dilemma in which the target of gaslighting finds herself. The question of with what conception of mental health and illness we *ought* to operate (the relevant ameliorative conception) is another question altogether—one touched on in section 6 of this chapter. For an exploration of the relationship between these two modes of evaluation (medical and moral), see my 2016/2017 article.

5. Strawson, 1974, 9–10.

is the case, and what she ought to do, and responsible for her failures to do so. These "reactive attitudes," as Strawson calls them, are attitudes through which we hold persons responsible for their good or ill will (or conduct, or intentions). Anger, for instance, is experienced not just as a response to someone's wrongdoing but as making a demand *of* the wrongdoer—for apology, reparation, explanation.[6] In this sense, our attitudes toward a person whom we regard as psychologically unwell aren't just different from but deeply opposed to our attitudes toward those whom we regard as responsible. And so it is that when faced with someone we think seriously mentally ill, we find ourselves saying things like, "You shouldn't be angry with her; she's not in her right mind."[7]

In this light, the fact that gaslighters frame their targets as "crazy" or "paranoid" is already telling, for these are ways of framing the target of gaslighting such that she cannot be a source of genuine challenge. Someone who is insane isn't, insofar as they are insane, in a position to issue proper challenges to anyone's views and in that respect presents no threat to the gaslighter who is unable to tolerate being challenged. In this sense, gaslighters create a comforting fantasy for themselves by framing their targets as crazy—she's paranoid, crazy, oversensitive; her basic rational capacities have escaped her, so nothing she says can count as protest, objection, or counterevidence of which the gaslighter ought to take account.[8] That basic fantasy

6. On this point, see esp. Darwall, 2009.

7. The general point at issue here is one that Strawson himself makes.

8. I'm setting aside cases where the gaslighter's motives are fully conscious to him, and his sayings of such things as "you're crazy" are simply lies. That difference doesn't matter for present purposes. What matters here is how the gaslighter's claims that his target is "crazy," "imagining things," etc. work on her.

can then serve other psychological needs of the gaslighter, such as a need to see the target as like a young child who needs someone to take over for her. Think, for instance, of Collier's squeezing Pat's shoulders and saying, "Why don't you just let me take charge!"

On the other hand, it's not clear that gaslighters are entirely convinced by their own fantasies. First, as we just noted, when the gaslighter says such things to their targets, they do so in that odd if familiar way that simultaneously implies that their targets are both out of their minds and yet somehow still blameworthy for it. We'll return to that in a moment. The other feature of gaslighting behavior that raises doubts about whether or how deeply gaslighters are convinced by their fantasy about the target's being "paranoid," "crazy," "out of her mind" is the fact that they work very hard to *try to make those fantasies real* by devoting themselves, over substantial periods of time, to undermining their targets as deliberators and moral agents.[9]

9. Given that we're talking about people whose motives are commonly not entirely conscious, the question of whether they're convinced by their own fantasies is inevitably one about the interpretation of mostly unconscious motives. On one common psychoanalytic view, people often act to make real that of which they are already unconsciously convinced, like the patient who acts so as to ensure the world is as disappointing as she's sure it is (Lear, 2011). But there are other ways of interpreting such cases consistent with psychoanalytic principles. Perhaps the person is desperately *fearful* that that is how the world works and acts so as to make the fantasy real, hoping that the world will, as it were, "push back." Or perhaps the person desperately *wants* the world to be as she fantasizes it is, and so she acts so as to make that fantasy real. It's this last possibility that I suspect is the usual case with gaslighters. But the crucial point is that whatever interpretation we offer of gaslighters at this level, the core fact remains—they call their targets "crazy" and then act so as *to make that* in some sense true.

Very often, moreover, one of the first steps gaslighters take toward trying to make that fantasy a reality is actually saying things like "that's crazy" or "you're being paranoid" or "that never happened" or "there's no pattern!" *to* the target. But why? Why does it make sense, from the gaslighter's perspective, to do that? And why, from the perspective of the target, do remarks like these play such an important (and afterward memorable) role in undermining her?

It's important to bear in mind at this juncture that targets of gaslighting don't recognize that they're being gaslit while it's going on—that's part of how and why this works.[10] So consider what you would think if someone responded to you by saying "that's crazy," "you're imagining things," or "don't be paranoid." It would, of course, matter *who* said this to you and in what relationship you stand to them. But even in a relatively impersonal relationship like one of workplace colleagues, there's going to be some conversational pressure to take what they say seriously enough to wonder whether you've said something so off base as to have deserved such a response. After all, if the person saying this to you *really* thought you're *so* crazy, paranoid, or delusional as to be beyond the reach of reasoning, it's hard to see what point there could be in his saying such a thing *to you*. A reasonable person, faced with someone saying such a thing to them, is apt—at least initially—to treat it as a harshly intoned prompt to rethink how one views the situation. Or, to put it another way, a reasonable person will treat "that's crazy" or "don't be paranoid" as a claim about the evidence or about what reasons there are, and respond

10. Recall discussion of this point in chapter 4.

accordingly. And typically, they do. Paula responds to Gregory's insistence that she's lost the brooch he'd given her (and that this is evidence she's losing her mind) by giving specifics about putting it in her purse. Similarly, in one of our examples from chapter 2, the target initially responds to an attempt at racist gaslighting about police violence by citing "case after case and story after story of inappropriate treatment." And in yet another example from earlier in the book, the target responds to being told that her views are crazy by citing evidence of a shared view: "It's not crazy to think so. I'm not the only one who thinks this, so does...."

All of these are attempts on the part of the targets of gaslighting to treat utterances like "that's crazy," "you're being paranoid," and "you're imagining things" as claims about the evidence and invitations (albeit obnoxious ones) to reason together. But because it's in fact gaslighting that's going on, there's no genuine uptake of the target's efforts to reason together—that was never the gaslighter's goal, after all. This refusal of uptake can take any number of forms, depending in part on the relationship between gaslighter and target. In the example of racist gaslighting about police violence, for instance, the gaslighters responded by just re-entrenching, insisting that the target(s) are "merely imagining it." In the case of the target of gaslighting who defended herself by noting that someone else shared her views, the gaslighter responded simply, "Well then, he's crazy too." In the scene from *Pat and Mike* we discussed earlier, Collier responds to Pat's efforts *simply to make room for her to reason*—that is, "I have to have time to think it over"—with the straight-out emotional blackmail of opening the newspaper, thereby literally and metaphorically shutting her out. And when, in yet another example from chapter 2, Liz's boss responds to her efforts to discuss problematic events by recommending that she "take a few days off to destress," the manipulative move is slightly different, but equally clear—her job is on the line, and this is not to be the subject of conversation.

Responses like these on the part of the gaslighter perform three important kinds of work for him. First, they encourage the target to give up trying to argue with the gaslighter. Second, they confuse the situation from the target's perspective—on the one hand, it looks like the gaslighter is saying things the most reasonable interpretation of which is that they are prompts to reason together; on the other hand, the gaslighter refuses to take up any of the target's efforts to reason together. And third, and equally key here, these responses involve the gaslighter exerting interpersonal emotional pressure on their target to accept the gaslighter's framing of the situation. This could be anything from the fear of losing one's job that Liz's boss deliberately elicits to Collier's attempt to goad Pat with his emotional shutout, appeals to empathy, or even appeals to the target's fears of losing the love of the gaslighter (Gregory is a master at this last technique in sometimes subtle ways, but much simpler tactics, like simply yelling at the target "how dare you say that!" in response to her efforts to reason together can communicate the same threat). The combination of these three facets of prototypical interactions with a gaslighter, especially insofar as they are iterated over time, is an especially effective form of manipulation.

In the most general sense, the kind of manipulation that's at issue here is what's sometimes called emotional goading—that is a form of manipulation that relies on influencing the target's emotional states. But even within that subset of manipulative conduct, what's at issue here is extremely unusual, and we're now in a position to start naming the idiosyncrasies of the form of manipulation at issue in gaslighting to which I earlier alluded. First, there's the fact that the goading at issue is a push toward two deeply conflicting affective states. On the one hand, there's the push toward the kind of radical self-doubt about one's own sanity that would be appropriate for someone who is genuinely, in the medical sense, "paranoid" or "imagining things," a push that's reinforced by the fact that the gaslighter refuses to engage with the target's reasons *as* reasons. On the other hand, there's the push toward feeling the guilt and/or shame of a responsible agent who isn't "crazy" or "paranoid" but is, in a looser, collo-quial sense, "acting crazy" or "acting paranoid" and so properly subject to moral condemnation. The strange emotional goading involved in gaslighting works only if you have both sides of this affective equation in play. Take away the push toward radical self-doubt concerning one's own sanity and all one has is an ordinary guilt trip. Take away the condemnation, and one takes away the target's sense that there is something she could do, should have done, could be doing, to end the torment—a sense that, as we've seen (in chapter 4), is key to making the target blame-lessly complicit in her own undoing. In gaslighting, the emo-tional goading involves both sides of this affective equation, and the fact that that's so then brings an additional kind of manipula-tive move into play. That is, in the context of gaslighting, some-thing like "don't be paranoid" involves a tacit no-win emotional choice point. It frames the target's options as either (1) accept the claim of wrongdoing ("acting as though paranoid") as well as the demand for apology, reparation implied by the gaslighter's anger about this, *or* (2) accept a view of oneself as (insofar as the matter at hand is concerned) not a morally responsible agent but the proper object of "treatment or management." The emotional manipulation involved in gaslighting induces the target to experience these as her only real options, to thereby accept the gaslighter's framing of the situation, and in that specific sense to be emotionally goaded into agreeing with her tormentor.

A second unusual aspect of the manipulative dimensions of gaslighting is that like some—but not all—forms of manipulation, this aspect of gaslighting works in part by disguising itself for what it is. People who are successfully gaslit don't know it's going on at the time. Guilt-tripping is a good contrast case here—we're all familiar with the experience of being successfully guilt-tripped, even as we fully recognize that that's what's going on. Third, unlike many forms of manipulation, gaslighting has to be iterated over time in order to be successful. You cannot fundamentally undermine someone's deliberative abilities and moral agency in a single interpersonal exchange. A great deal of manipulative conduct that makes use of emotional goading isn't like that. Fourth, a lot of emotional manipulation is aimed at getting someone to do something in particular (call, do something, or even just "pay attention to the manipulator"). Gaslighting, in contrast, is properly grouped with those forms of manipulation that are aimed at changing or controlling underlying affective and evaluative dispositions—for example, Iago's aim of getting Othello to view Desdemona with deep and general suspicion, the bully who tries to manipulate others into viewing him as a victim, the mean girl who aims to be seen as damsel in distress, and so forth. But fifth, as we've seen over and over again, even within that subset, the aim of gaslighting is uniquely extreme. The gaslighter isn't trying to manipulate you into having a different evaluative or deliberative perspective; the characteristic gaslighting desire, as we've seen, is to destroy the possibility of disagreement, where the only sure path to that is destroying the source of possible disagreement—the independent, separate, deliberative perspective from which disagreement might arise.

With these differences between gaslighting and other forms of manipulation laid bare, it's immediately clear how implausible it is to suppose that whatever makes gaslighting wrong, and whatever that wrongness consists in, it's simply to be read off of "whatever the wrong-making feature of wrongful manipulation is."[11]

Nevertheless, as I suggested at the beginning of this section, some common views about what's wrong with manipulation can help us articulate the wrongs of gaslighting, by allowing us to highlight the ways in which the wrongs of gaslighting *understood as a form of manipulation* differ from the wrongs of other forms of manipulation. Consider, for instance, the common view that what's wrong with manipulation is that it interferes with people's right to make their own decisions, their rights of self-government.[12] Thoughts along these lines are very much a part of everyday discourse. For instance, people who've been

11. Stark, 2019.

12. See, e.g., Hill, 1984; O'Neill, 1990; Korsgaard, 1986. My own way of elucidating the claim that ordinary manipulation violates people's rights to govern themselves is less metaphysical than the accounts of some of these authors. This is partly a matter of my own philosophical predilections and partly because what's needed here is a way of understanding this objection that can capture the sort of thing people say in everyday life when they are objecting to being manipulated without importing unnecessary metaphysical baggage.

manipulated often object by saying things like "you know I wouldn't have agreed to this if you'd told me the truth" or "stop trying to get me to do what you want by guilting me!" One way of spelling out the underlying objection at issue in such cases is to say that manipulation interferes with a person's right to self-govern by objectionably inducing them to act in ways, and/or for reasons they do not reflectively endorse. I'm not especially interested in pursuing whether we can capture what's wrong with ordinary manipulation in these terms, though it strikes me as a plausible account of at least part of what's wrong with such behavior.[13] What's more interesting for our purposes is how woefully inadequate this is as an account of the way in which gaslighting interferes with the target's right to govern themselves. The gaslighter isn't simply trying to induce someone to act in ways or for reasons they would not endorse on reflection. The gaslighter is attempting to interfere with their target's right to govern herself by trying to undercut the target's *ability* to govern herself.[14]

Here's a second common view about what's wrong with manipulation: manipulating someone wrongs them by failing

13. In this respect I disagree with Buss, 2005, though nothing in my argument concerning gaslighting hangs on this.

14. It's interesting to note in this light that Buss, in the course of arguing that it's not plausible to think that what's wrong with what I'm calling ordinary manipulation is that it interferes with an individual's right to self-government, writes, "In fact, however, there are limits to what most manipulators are willing to do to their victims, . . . In particular: someone who intends to manipulate another human being would not necessarily be willing to destroy, or even disable, this person's capacity for autonomous choice; nor would he necessarily be willing to prevent her from exercising this capacity" (2005, 216). The contrast on this score between what Buss thinks is true of "most manipulators" and what we've seen is true of gaslighters is vivid.

to accord them the respect they are owed, simply in virtue of being a person.[15] This is almost always fleshed out in terms of our obligation to respect persons' rights to self-government, making this fundamental disrespect the necessary concomitant to the violations of self-government involved in manipulating someone. But if we're talking about gaslighting, there's more to say in two respects. First, recall our overview above of how the emotional goading involved in gaslighting works and the reasons phrases like "that's crazy" and "don't be paranoid" play such an important role therein. A key part of the process is goading the target to adopt two conflicting emotional attitudes toward herself, one of which involves deeply doubting her own sanity (here: her own basic deliberative abilities and practical/moral agency). She is being induced, thereby, to regard herself through the lens of what Strawson calls "the objective attitude"—as "the proper object of treatment, management," rather than as someone with whom one can reason, who can be held responsible—a member of the moral community. To this extent, and in this respect, gaslighters not only frame their targets as outside the moral community but induce their targets to so view *themselves*. Viewing an individual who is part of the moral community as though she is not a member is fundamentally disrespectful.

15. See, e.g., Hill, 1980. It's not surprising that Hill should appear both here and in the earlier footnote in this chapter that lists philosophers who take the view that what's wrong with manipulation is that it interferes with people's right to make their own decisions, their rights of self-government. In fact all of the authors cited in that footnote also see manipulation as a failure of basic respect, precisely *because* (they argue) it involves violating the target's rights to self-government.

There's another dimension to the disrespect involved in gaslighting that's distinctive, having to do with the fact that successful gaslighting occurs over time. Suppose, for the moment, that all manipulative conduct involves failures of respect. In many cases, the manipulator's disrespect is apt to be a relatively short-lived objectionable attitude—a slip of sorts, if you will—in someone who usually has decent enough regard for the person whom they manipulated. The gaslighter's disrespect for their target cannot be momentary in that way. Because gaslighting takes place over time—paradigmatically, long stretches of time—the gaslighter's disrespect for their target has to be a durable and consistent enough aspect of how they are *disposed* to regard that person to play its role in motivating the gaslighter over and over again. This is more than a passing bad attitude; it's a matter of bad character.

A third way that the wrongs of manipulation are sometimes understood is under the general rubric of pretense or deception.[16] Of course, manipulation in general and gaslighting in particular frequently involve straightforward deception. More interesting examples, however, involve the kind of deception that can occur through those forms of emotional goading that make use of reactive attitudes.[17] In these cases, what's at issue

16. In a way, Herman (1993) holds this view, but that's because she thinks that deception and manipulation are both wrong in that they violate (and in the same way) persons' right to self-government. There's another way of thinking about the connection between manipulation and deceit on which what's wrong with manipulation just *is* that it's a form of deception. Sometimes, after all, "you lied!" is a perfectly sufficient account of what's wrong with what someone did.

17. Darwall is, I think, pointing in the direction of the kind of surreptitious pretense I have in mind here—a pretense that can be created through manipulative

is more pretense than classic deception, and it's a pretense that works through the implicit evaluative presentation of the reactive attitudes. When I am angry with someone, my anger is a kind of lens through which I see them as having done something wrong, and an emotion that I experience as directed *at* them in a way that expects something (e.g., apology) *of* them.[18] So when the manipulator goads through anger (as, for instance, Gregory often does with Paula), the target (reasonably) experiences his anger as making a kind of claim—that she has wronged him—and as making a demand of her—for apology, reparation, explanation. But, of course, in the cases we're talking about, there is no wrongdoing; the pretense is a false one.

Gaslighting is thus not only interpersonally but also morally very different from other forms of manipulation. To begin with, the emotional goading implicated in gaslighting is unusual in the five respects enumerated above. Of those five, the most significant is the fact that the particular kind of emotional goading that is characteristic of gaslighting—that which is involved in the gaslighter's use of accusations like "that's crazy," "you're being paranoid," "there's no pattern"—works by placing its target in an awful emotional catch-22. The target is goaded into experiencing herself as having the choice between seeing herself as "crazy" in the sense of being a proper object of "treatment

---

use of the reactive attitudes—when he writes that some forms of manipulation "purport to create reasons in something like the way that legitimate claims or demands do, that is, second-personally, but without the appropriate normative backing for the threatened 'sanctions,' which consequently provide only the superficial appearance of an accountability relation" (2009, 51).

18. Think of the way that fear, similarly, presents its object as dangerous even when one knows that the object is not dangerous.

and management" rather than reasoning, or seeing herself as "acting as though crazy" in the sense of acting in ways that are utterly outrageous and blameworthy and for which she therefore owes the gaslighter an apology, reparations, and so on.[19]

We've seen that there's also a significant contrast between the way in which ordinary manipulation violates someone's rights of self-government and the way that gaslighting does so. Ordinary manipulation interferes with people's right to govern themselves by inducing them to act in ways, or for reasons, they would not reflectively endorse. Gaslighting interferes with people's right to govern themselves by undermining the basic deliberative, evaluative, and practical capacities required to govern oneself.

And we've seen that there are important differences between the disrespect involved in ordinary manipulation and that which is implicated in gaslighting. Ordinary manipulation involves failing to treat a person with the respect she is owed as a person—a fellow member of the moral community—in that it interferes with her rights to self-governance and that's disrespectful. While gaslighting is disrespectful in this way as well, the form of disrespect involved in gaslighting also has all the following features: (1) Gaslighting interferes with an individual's rights of self-governance in a much more serious fashion than ordinary manipulation—its aim is to undermine its target's basic deliberative capacity and moral agency. Accordingly, the

19. The "therefore" in this sentence is important. There may be cases in which we think (perhaps appropriately) that, although not morally responsible, the agent should apologize, or offer reparations of some sort (cases of blameless wrongdoing and/or what Williams called agent regret, Williams, 1981). Here, in contrast, it's crucial that part of what the gaslighter is trying to do is induce in his target the sense that she should apologize *because* she's blameworthy.

disrespect it involves is more serious. (2) Gaslighters frame their targets as "crazy," "paranoid," and so on. One effect of this is that they thereby frame their targets as the proper objects of "treatment and management" rather than responsible moral agents. This too is fundamentally disrespectful. (3) Gaslighters attempt to induce their targets to *see themselves* as proper objects of "treatment and management." (4) To succeed, gaslighting must take place over a long stretch of time. The disrespectful attitudes held by the gaslighter, accordingly, cannot be one-off slips but must instead be durable aspects of the gaslighter's attitudes toward his target.

2. The Epistemic Wrongs of Gaslighting

There are, of course, significant epistemic dimensions to the wrongs of gaslighting. After all, one of the gaslighter's central aims is to undermine the target's basic deliberative abilities. However, some of the recent literature on gaslighting makes misleading claims in this territory. Noticing where some such ideas go awry will help us get clearer about what we *are* talking about when we talk about the epistemic wrongs of gaslighting.

There are three claims some have made about the epistemic wrongs of gaslighting that are to my mind importantly misguided. The first two can be treated together. (1) The wrongs of gaslighting are fundamentally epistemic, or, slightly more weakly, (2) the wrongs of gaslighting are most importantly epistemic wrongs.[20] There's a tangle of difficulties with such

---

20. In fact, it's sometimes not quite clear which of these two claims an author intends. Fortunately, for our purposes here, it doesn't matter. See, e.g., McKinnon, 2017; Podosky, 2021.

claims. To begin with, there's the fact that most of the common contexts in which gaslighting occurs are not only practical but specifically moral arenas—for example, gaslighting as a response to protests against injustice, spousal gaslighting with specific relational aims such as Collier's gaslighting Pat with the aim of getting her to abandon her career, gaslighting in response to interpersonal wrongdoing. It's hard to see why one would be even tempted to think that the wrongs of gaslighting in contexts such as these can be captured fundamentally or primarily as ways in which someone is wronged in their capacity to know or form justified beliefs. Take the case of Pat and Collier. We could describe some of Collier's gaslighting aims in epistemic terms—for example, he wants to radically undermine her ability to deliberate well about her golfing abilities. But the business about golf in particular is really a sideshow in Collier's motivational psychology. His core gaslighting aim is to radically undermine Pat's ability to decide what she wants for her life, so that she'll give up, defer to him, and devote herself to the wifely endeavors Collier has in mind. The ability or skill of self-determination that Collier aims to undermine certainly involves epistemic skills (self-discernment, notably), but it is not, in the first instance, an epistemic ability. Or consider any of the cases in which the gaslighting arises as a response to the target's protest against injustice or wrongdoing. To say that the wrong involved in those cases is primarily epistemic would be misleading. Of course, part of what the gaslighter aims to undermine in such cases is the agent's moral knowledge— for example, her knowledge that she's been wronged, that an injustice has been committed, and/or that discrimination is afoot. But in cases like these, the target's moral *agency* is at least as much the focus of the gaslighter's destructive aims as her epistemic capacities. After all, it is her protests against injustice to which he responded with gaslighting, and if anything is a core exercise in moral agency, surely protesting against injustice belongs in that category.

Perhaps we could imagine a case in which the gaslighter takes aim exclusively or primarily at the target's epistemic abilities, and not such practical abilities as deciding what one wants, or specifically moral skills like responding in morally apt ways to wrongdoing. But none of the cases of gaslighting that are commonly agreed to be paradigmatic are like that, and none of the cases we've discussed in this book are like that.

A third misguided claim about the epistemic wrongs of gaslighting that's gained some traction is the thought that insofar as gaslighting does involve specifically epistemic wrongs, we should understand those wrongs as epistemic *injustices* and, even more particularly, as matters of what Miranda Fricker coined "testimonial injustice."[21] Some cases of gaslighting do involve injustice. As we've seen, it is not infrequently the case that gaslighters focus their efforts on members of marginalized populations, and oppressive social norms associated with various forms of systematic oppression (racism, sexism, heterosexism, classism) can be used as tools by gaslighters in a variety of ways. But not all cases of gaslighting implicate matters of injustice: a straight white woman can gaslight her straight white husband, and do so in ways that fit every canonical description of gaslighting. Though that is profoundly wrong, it is not a

---

21. See, e.g., McKinnon, 2017; Spear, 2023; McGlynn, 2020; Bailey, 2020; Podosky, 2021.

matter of injustice. Moreover, the ways in which injustice is implicated in gaslighting when it is implicated are not specifically epistemic, as opposed to practical or moral. The sexist appeal (in one of our examples in chapter 2) for a woman to "have some sympathy" for the guy who slapped her on the butt is just as much aimed at undermining with whom she sympathizes, what she is motivated to do, and in what manner as it is aimed at undermining her confidence that the guy with whom she's told to sympathize did something wrong.

While the wrongs of gaslighting do not always include epistemic injustices, there's an important lesson for us in considering one version of the claim that they do—the claim that gaslighting is an instance of what Fricker calls "testimonial injustice."[22] Testimonial injustice has to do with the ways in which a speaker's credibility is assessed. It occurs when a person who is a member of a marginalized group makes a claim that she intends to be taken as testimony—she intends that we take her "at her word" we'd say colloquially—but her claim is not taken as seriously (it is afforded less credence) than it would otherwise be, precisely because she is a member of a socially marginalized group.[23] By contrast, gaslighting aims to put questions of credibility off the table entirely. The gaslighter is trying to turn a situation that might otherwise involve credibility assessments into a situation in which credibility assessments are not at issue, because there is no *credibility* to be assessed, no other perspective in the offing, and so no possibility of disagreement. Remember, part of what's distinctive about gaslighting is that the gaslighter isn't satisfied

22. The first to make this particular claim was McKinnon, 2017.
23. Fricker, 2007, 28.

with merely framing the target in his own mind as "crazy." He tries to make that framing real by radically undermining her basic competencies as deliberator and moral agent—the very competencies that allow her to occupy an independent standpoint and that are partly constitutive of that standpoint. To the extent he succeeds, he ensures that the target occupies no independent standpoint from which she might issue (more or less credible) challenges to his views or perspective.[24]

One theme we can see emerging here is that the epistemic and non-epistemic wrongs of gaslighting are inextricably tied up with one another. This is true both as a practical matter and analytically. The practical entanglement can be seen by thinking through an example. Consider this one from Myisha Cherry:

An undergrad witnesses racist behavior from his teacher's assistant. Being quite angry with the TA, the student sets up a meeting with the TA to discuss the matter. The TA responds to the angry complaint by saying, "You are imagining that what I said was racist. My behavior wasn't that bad. If you were not a sensitive snow-flake who gets crazy ideas of racism from the media, we would not be having this conversation." He then says to the undergrad that he understands that being the only Arab American student in class may make him sensitive to issues of race but he assures the student, "You have nothing to really be angry or worried about. Everyone is not out to get you."[25]

24. We might say that her utterances can then be treated as evidence but not testimony, following Moran's helpful way of drawing that distinction (Moran, 2018).

25. Cherry, 2017, 61.

If this incident is aimed at undermining this person's own sense of standing to experience the reactive attitude of anger (especially anger in response to racism), and ability to deliberate in relevant ways about her own anger, then we've got a case of gaslighting. If, as a result of a pattern of such incidents, one comes to view one's own anger as illegitimate (either in general, or with regard to some specific arena like anger about racism), one will to that extent take it that all the evaluatively laden ways in which one's anger presents the world are similarly illegitimate. This includes, notably, the fact that anger presents the world as one in which someone has been wronged. That one's evaluative capacities are, in this way, undermined is a necessary concomitant to viewing one's own anger as generally illegitimate. And that's a significant epistemic dimension to the way that gaslighting works in a case like this. But having one's sense of title to be angry undermined will also undermine moral agency. If one doesn't ever feel that one's anger is legitimate, then one will not experience the moral demands that are part and parcel of the experience of anger—demands for apology, contrition, reparation—as legitimate either. And a core part of seeing oneself as a moral agent—as part of a community of mutually accountable individuals—is seeing oneself as entitled to sometimes make such demands for accountability. To the extent that is undermined, so is one's sense of oneself as a moral agent.[26] Moreover, one's sense of one's own

26. One needn't be committed to a reactive attitude-centered account of blame to see that this is true. Even someone like Scanlon can grant that well-functioning adults treat negative reactive attitudes as defeasibly reliable guides to when wrongdoing has occurred and what is appropriately demanded by way of apology, contrition, etc. in light of that wrongdoing, and come to *rely* on the reliability of these

value will also thereby be undermined. Our sense of our own *value* as individuals is inextricably bound up with our sense of ourselves as having standing to protest with anger, indignation, resentment; radically undermine the latter and you radically undermine the former. And there will be other devastating downstream effects, some of them implicating other aspects of the target's deliberative capacities. Here's one example. People who come to view their own anger as illegitimate do not thereby eliminate their anger. Instead, what happens is that the anger either gets directed inward and turns into clinical depression or is deflected—sideways, as it were—onto inappropriate targets. And each of these effects, in turn, tends to lead to distortions in the agent's deliberative abilities.

In nearly every case of gaslighting, its epistemic dimensions are tied up in a complicated web like this with other kinds of wrongs to the person's sense of her own standing as a moral agent, her ability to exercise the skills constitutive of moral agency (like holding others accountable), and her sense of her own value. In part, as the TA example shows, this is a practical matter about the way that gaslighting works in creatures who have psychologies like ours. But this kind of entanglement of the epistemic and non-epistemic is also close

---

attitudes as such guides. Thus, even if one supposes, with Scanlon, that it's *conceptually* possible to specify both the appropriate conditions for blame and the content of blame without reference to the reactive attitudes, the fact of our reliance on the reactive attitudes as moral guides is going to mean that someone who is induced to see all her anger as illegitimate is someone who is going to have her ability to make judgments about wrongdoing radically undermined. For an argument that suggests Scanlon would find this line of reasoning unobjectionable, see his 2012 chapter.

to an analytic truth about gaslighting, given (1) the kinds of basic skills and abilities that the gaslighter aims to undermine in her target and (2) the kinds of dispositions the gaslighter uses as tools in pursuit of her aims. Some of the gaslighter's tools might seem to be primarily epistemic—for example, the appeal to the working assumption of deliberation and conversation, "I might be wrong." Others might seem to be primarily practical and/or moral—such as appeals to trust and empathy. But as we noted in chapter 4, in fact, all eight of the most important implements in the gaslighter's toolbox in fact play foundational roles in both our practical and our epistemic lives.

The same basic point can be made about the damage that gaslighting does when it is successful. You cannot shred someone's basic deliberative abilities without doing at least as much damage to them as a moral agent, and vice versa. If you make a mess of someone's trusting dispositions, you make a mess of both their epistemic and moral skills. So too with regard to the clinical consequences of gaslighting (see also the final section of this chapter): it would be bizarre to ask whether clinical depression is more undermining of one's ability to form justified beliefs or else one's ability to act well and virtuously.

In this respect as well, gaslighting's immorality is unusual. The wrongs of gaslighting aren't solely or most fundamentally epistemic; they're not solely or most fundamentally something other than epistemic (moral, practical). But neither are they *merely* a combination of epistemic and moral or practical wrongs. In at least some respects—those we've just been talking about—the wrongs of gaslighting outstrip and are prior to such distinctions.

3. The Wrongs of the Gaslighter's Tools

Gaslighters also wrong their targets in ways that have to do specifically with the tools they use as means to gaslighting and the manner in which they use those tools. To see this clearly, it's useful to divide the tools gaslighters commonly use (discussed individually in chapter 4) into two overlapping categories. In the first category are dispositions that, in a variety of ways, play essential and fundamental roles in our lives. There are dispositions in this category that are critical to our deliberative capacities and/or moral agency, those through which we orient ourselves toward the world and other people, and those that play foundational roles in the ways in which we organize our individual lives and find meaning in them. This is a diverse category that includes everything from the defeasible presumption of fallibility ("I might be wrong") to trust, love, empathy, our desire for the company of others, our need for interpersonal confirmation, and our practical and emotional investment in the significant life projects (e.g., work or family life) that we find most meaningful. When gaslighters use dispositions in this category as tools, they do so in ways that rely on the normative structure and significance of these dispositions.

In some cases, this involves relying on the fact that having one of these dispositions gives us, or seems to us to give us, *reasons* to do certain things, react in certain ways, and so forth. Trusting someone, for instance, doesn't just prompt us to give their views (with respect to the arenas of trust) extra credence; rather, the experience of trusting someone seems to give us *reasons* to give their views a bit more credence.[27] Gaslighters' appeals to their target's trust often rely on this.

In other cases, gaslighters rely on the normative significance that the disposition they use as a tool has for us. We value the presence of these dispositions in our lives. We value the ability to trust and to love, we value having people in our lives whom we trust and love, we think that it's appropriate to presume that we might be wrong and be motivated by that presumption because we value the truth. When gaslighters use any of these dispositions as tools, they rely not simply on their target having the disposition in question but also on the fact that she values having that disposition. One way to see this is by way of contrast. Imagine, for instance, someone who has concluded that although she does indeed tend to work under the presumption of fallibility—and so questions her assumptions, listens to counterarguments, rechecks her reasoning—she shouldn't, because the truth just doesn't matter enough (she doesn't value it enough) to care about whether or not she's wrong.[28] For someone like that, hearing the gaslighter say "that didn't happen" or "there's no pattern" would be a bit like jumping out of bed early to dress for work only to realize it's Saturday—one would feel drawn to doubt oneself, but then lose any such temptation once one realized one simply didn't care whether one was wrong.[29]

27. Under what conditions trust in fact gives us such reasons, and what we can learn about those conditions from gaslighting, is one of the topics of discussion in chapter 7.

28. See, e.g., Donald Trump or Harry Frankfurt's "bullshitter."

29. Of course matters can be more complicated than this. Even someone who didn't endorse her standing presumption of fallibility might find it "sticky" in such a way that the presumption motivates her in spite of her rejection of it.

To get you to doubt yourself, the gaslighter counts on you having an investment in getting to the truth of the matter, an investment that justifies having and maintaining a working presumption that you might be wrong, which in turn can motivate self-doubt in the face of the gaslighter's counter-claims or purported evidence.

In a third set of cases, the normative feature on which the gaslighter relies is the fact that some of these dispositions can be a *source* of valuing. Consider, for instance, some of the ways in which gaslighters weaponize love.[30] When a gaslighter who is beloved by his target manipulates her by insinuating (or stating) that her opposition pains him, he is relying on her valuing him and his well-being in the way that loving someone gives us reason to value them.

In all three kinds of cases, gaslighters rely on the normative dimensions of dispositions that play essential roles in our lives as deliberators and moral agents. Some of those dispositions, like the working presumption that one might be wrong, are directly implicated in our deliberative capacities and moral agency. Others of these dispositions are indirectly implicated in our deliberative abilities and moral agency because the dispositions themselves are crucial to how we organize our lives and find meaning in them through our valuing capacities. In short, gaslighters use dispositions that are crucial to our lives as deliberators and moral agents in order to radically undermine their targets as deliberators and moral agents. Put slightly differently, gaslighters make use of dispositions that play crucial

---

30. For two contrasting views, both of which hold that loving is a source and mode of valuing, see Frankfurt, 2004, and Abramson and Leite, 2018.

roles in our lives as creatures who value, in order to undermine our ability to appropriately value. If anything counts as moral perversity, it's that.

The second of the two overlapping categories of the gas-lighter's tools worth singling out here are those whose use by the gaslighter has pernicious political and social dimensions. The paradigmatic examples of this are oppressive social norms and stereotypes (women are hysterical, Black people are overly angry, etc.), which, as we saw in chapter 4, are especially effectively weaponized as tools insofar as they have been in-ternalized by the targets of gaslighting. There are three spe-cifically political dimensions to the gaslighter's wrongdoings insofar as these are his tools. First, the immoral use of already pernicious social structures—the use of oppressive social norms in the service of gaslighting—is a political choice, for which the gaslighter is blameworthy. Second, to choose this kind of tool as a tool of gaslighting is to compound the dam-age of gaslighting in a specifically politically laden way by reinforcing—for the target, with respect to herself—the very oppressive social norm that the gaslighter has chosen as tool, and thereby limit (yet further) the psychologically real possibilities for the target going forward. For instance, the gaslighter who makes manipulative use of the trope that "women are hysterical" in order to induce a woman to see her-self as hysterical limits her possibilities in a way that's specifi-cally tied to that very oppressive social norm. And third, using oppressive social norms as tools in gaslighting, particularly insofar as the gaslighting is successful, is also a pernicious political act insofar as it constitutes a moment of preserving and reinforcing larger structures of injustice.

4. Blameless Complicity

As we saw in chapter 4, gaslighting is like torture in that it makes us complicit in our own suffering. Here too, however, the wrongs of gaslighting are distinctive. Two differences between torture and gaslighting are especially important. Torture and gaslighting have in common that, as Sussman says about torture, they force their target into a position "of colluding against himself through his own affects and emotions, so that he experiences himself as simultaneously powerless and yet actively complicit in his own violation."[31] In torture, it is canonically pain—and paradigmatically physical pain—that presents itself to us in ways that we experience as colluding with our tormenter. The pain the torturer causes is inflicted on its victim and experienced by her in *that* sense as alien to her, as happening to her rather than *of* her. And yet, at the same time, "insofar as the experience of pain has any content, it seems to be that of a pure imperative." "To feel pain," Sussman notes, "is to confront something like a bodily demand to change something about one's condition, to do something to silence this very demand."[32] Try to imagine experiencing even something so simple as the pain of a hand on a hot stove and *not* experiencing that pain as demanding that one remove one's hand from the stove. In this way, whatever else is going on in torture, the pain the torturer inflicts seems to take his side, colluding against the tortured and demanding that one give the torturer what he wants.

31. Sussman, 2005, 4.
32. Sussman, 2005, 20.

The way in which we are brought to collude against ourselves in gaslighting is quite different. As we've seen both in chapter 4 and, in a different way, in the preceding section, in gaslighting it's centrally the basic *processes* by which one forms apt beliefs, doubts, and reactive responses, and one's *motivationally organizing* desires and affections (one's loves, central life endeavors, like work and family, one's basic empathetic capacities) that are made use of by the gaslighter and put one in a position of colluding against oneself. This difference with torture is significant. Most notably, the capacities through which the target of gaslighting is made to collude against herself are the very same capacities through which we create lives that have meaning to us as individuals, the capacities through which we create something that in Hume's terms is the "proper object of self-concern," or what Frankfurt famously coined "the dear self." Insofar as I am concerned for myself, after all, it is not just a concern for the continued existence of this body but also centrally a concern to nurture my loves, my interests, my endeavors, and my ability to discern and decide what shall be my loves, interests, and endeavors. These are the very dispositions through which the gaslighter makes the target complicit in her own undoing.

A second difference between torture and gaslighting is closely linked to this first. In plain terms, what the canonical torturer wants is some piece of information—that you should release whatever secrets you bear or names you harbor. The gaslighter aims to undermine your basic abilities as deliberator and moral agent. In each case, then, when we find ourselves induced to collude with our tormentor, *these* are the aims with which we are being induced to collude. And there's morally significant differences between being made to collude in someone's effort to get information they'll then use for terrible purposes and on the other hand being made to collude in one's own undoing as deliberator and moral agent.

5. Ordinary and Extraordinary Silencing

"Silencing," as Rae Langton coined the term, has to do with the fact that some of the "things we do with words" are impossible for some people in some circumstances.[33] "Although the appropriate words are uttered, with the appropriate intention, the speaker fails to perform" the act that would otherwise be performed with those words.[34] Those acts are, in Langton's terms, "unspeakable" for people in those circumstances. So for example, prior to 2015 in most of the United States, two women could not perform the speech act of marrying one another, no matter what else was true of the circumstances under which they uttered "I do."[35] The law made it impossible for that utterance between two women to count as the act of marrying. The acts we perform with words in the sense that's relevant here include warning, ordering, prohibiting, promising, marrying, protesting.

Telling is also plausibly thought of as a speech act. When I *tell* you what time it is, I'm giving you a reason to believe that relies on you taking me to have performed that speech act—that of telling you. You will say to someone who asks why you believe

---

33. Langton, 1993, 315–316. "Things we do with words" is in quotes above because it is, of course, J. L. Austin's famous phrase. It's Austin to whom Langton herself turns to explicate the relevant notion of silencing.

34. Langton, 1993, 299.

35. Langton, 1993, 317.

thus and such is the time, "well, that's what she told me." Suppose, instead, you were simply passing by me on the street and heard me muttering to myself "shoot, shoot, shoot—five o'clock!" Hearing this, you run to your appointment thinking you're late and arrive out of breath, only to see that the clock reads four forty-five. When queried as to why you are out of breath, you respond, "I think I misunderstood something I overheard on my way here." You will not say, "She told me."[36]

In these terms, it's plausible to see gaslighters as trying to create the conditions under which their target's utterances, especially with regard to whatever was the initial arena of gaslighting, will not count as *tellings*. The gaslighter doesn't just want other people to think his target is wrong. He wants her protests framed as "oversensitive," "paranoid," "acting out," and "rants." The more he succeeds, the less she will be able to engage in the relevant acts of telling, of protesting, and so on. In Langton's terms, those will become for her "unspeakable acts"; he will have created the conditions for her silencing.

But the silencing involved in gaslighting is actually much worse than this. The gaslighter, remember, isn't just concerned with what people other than his target make of her. The gaslighter wants the target to *see herself in the terms he paints her*. Even worse, he wants to make the terms in which he paints her a reality by actually undermining her basic abilities as deliberator and moral agent. Insofar then as gaslighting is successful, it will undermine the target's ability to take her own words, thoughts, views, reactions, concerns as having the normative force and content they otherwise would. She may be angry or,

36. See, e.g., Moran, 2018.

if she can no longer muster that, hurt in response to a discriminatory act, but she will not be able to take her own reactions
seriously herself—to treat those attitudes, herself, in any of the
myriad ways in which it is appropriate to treat anyone's reactive
attitudes. Rather than, for instance, understanding her own
anger as a potentially justified response to wrongdoing, a response that issues forth demands for apology and contrition,
someone who has been successfully gaslit will see her own
anger as nothing more than a mental storm.[37] Successful gaslighting, in this way, involves what might be aptly thought of as
a kind of existential silencing.

6. Psychological Damage

It would be obscene to write about the wrongs of gaslighting
without talking about the psychological damage it causes.
When gaslighting works well, its target ends up feeling "carved
up," "nobody," lost. Or she may say with Beauvoir, "I'm no longer sure . . . even if I think at all." Like Beauvoir, the successfully gaslit person loses her sense of independent standing
and, for a time, even some of her ability to engage in the deliberations constitutive of that independent standing. In the
psychological literature, this final "stage," as it's sometimes
called, of gaslighting has a name: severe, major, clinical depression.[38] That's hardly surprising.

37. This is, of course, a substantially broader sense of "silencing" than Langton's,
though, for reasons indicated above, one that strikes me as apt in this context.

38. On the link between gaslighting and depression, see, e.g., Robin Stern (who
describes depression as the final stage of gaslighting both in her 2007 book and on
her blog, https://robinstern.com/how-to-identify-the-gaslight-effect/); McQuillan, 2021; Nall, 2020.

And yet it's important to be clear and a bit delicate about exactly what we're implying when we say that severe clinical depression is a common outcome of successful gaslighting. We talk often in everyday life of clinical states as ones that— insofar as they are clinical—are inappropriate responses. In this context, that's not a helpful way of thinking. At worst, thinking about clinical states this way might suggest that someone who has been driven to depression by gaslighting has failed to respond well in some manner we might reasonably have expected of her. The latter, I think, would be an outrageous insinuation. So let's distinguish two issues: First, is a person's psychological state such that psychological help would be a good idea? And second, is her psychological state a fitting response to her situation? Someone who is suffering in ways that meet the criteria for major clinical depression does need psychological help. But we should treat it as an open question whether her needing psychological help shows that her response is not fitting. Imagine, for instance, someone grieving the death of a child. Surely being unable to function in the world, to remember, to sleep, to keep track of the details of everyday life are not just understandable but fitting responses to so horrific a loss. That doesn't mean it might not also be helpful to a person facing that loss to get psychological help working through it.[39] Someone who has been gaslit has lost, albeit partially and temporarily, herself. And in various ways, her depressive responses to that situation are fitting—she is

---

39. I offer a parallel example about the moral salience of expressions of grief in my 2012 book chapter and discuss the possibility of depression as a term belonging to a mode of evaluation rather than as something on the order of a "natural kind" in further detail in my 2016/2017 article.

grieving; she's grieving the loss of her independent perspective, her ability to form and maintain her own reactions and perceptions, the loss of the friendships that became or turned out to be mere gaslighting relations, and her own largely blameless complicity in all of this. It may take her a very long time, and work, to come to see her symptomatically depressive reactions in these terms; like many forms of significant grief, it can take work and self-understanding that's not easily or immediately accessible to experience its manifestations as grief. But, devastating though it is, it is precisely that.[40]

There are several other significant reasons to so reframe the psychological harms of gaslighting. Doing so shifts our perspective from one in which we see a gaslit woman as a mere object of treatment—qua clinically depressed—to one in which we see her as an ongoing member of the moral community, grieving losses of insuperable value. One reason it's so important to reframe matters in this way when thinking about the wrongs of gaslighting is that, as we've seen, a key part of what the gaslighter himself is trying to do is get the target to see herself as the proper object of "treatment and management." Moreover, this way of reframing our understanding of what it means to say that severe depression is one kind of common psychological harm of being gaslit then allows us to see

---

40. I'm aware of ways in which the line I am adopting here touches on recent controversial changes in the *DSM* and its addition of "prolonged grief disorder." Those debates are too complex to permit full discussion here. Note, however, that much of the movement against the inclusion of "bereavement" as possibly (a form of) depression objects that this "pathologizes" grief. But "pathologize," as the objectors are using it, carries with it exactly the connotation to which I'm objecting— namely, that a condition that it would be helpful getting therapeutic aid in working through is also and for that reason not a fitting response to one's situation.

the depression itself, if in a peculiar way, as the last form of resistance to gaslighting. If the gaslit person can grieve the loss of herself, then in fact she is not entirely lost. Her depression is not then merely the outcome of the wrongs she has suffered and endured; it's a fitting evaluative response to that to which she has been subjected and the first signpost on the road back.

7. What's Wrong with Gaslighting

Here's a summary of the wrongs of gaslighting we've identified, grouped by general category:

- The wrongs of gaslighting, considered as a form of manipulation, are multiple and differ in important ways from those involved in other forms of manipulation. These include:
  - inducing the target to experience an emotional catch-22 in which she experiences herself as having the choice between seeing herself as "crazy" (beyond the reach of reason) or else seeing herself as a responsible agent appropriately blamed for conduct so outrageous it qualifies as "acting as though crazy"
  - interfering with the target's right to govern herself, by trying to radically undercut her ability to do so
  - in an ongoing way that speaks to the gaslighter's character, failing to respect the target as one ought to respect any person
  - inducing the target to adopt fundamentally disrespectful attitudes toward *herself*
  - engaging in the aforementioned wrongs in part through deception and pretense

- Epistemic and epistemic implicating wrongs of gaslighting:
  - aiming to radically undercut the target's deliberative abilities
  - framing the target as beyond the reach of reason in such a way that she cannot issue (more or less credible) challenges to him, and aiming to undermine her so radically that she in fact cannot do so
  - aiming to undermine dispositions that are fundamental to *both* the target's epistemic and moral capacities
- Wrongs involving the canonical tools of gaslighting:
  - using dispositions that are fundamental to our deliberative capacities, our moral agency, and our lives as valuing agents more generally as tools to undermine their targets as deliberators, moral agents, and creatures who value
  - using internalized oppressive social norms and stereotypes as tools to undermine their targets
- Gaslighters wrong their target by making her complicit in her own undoing as deliberator and moral agent. To do this, gaslighters make use of the basic *processes* by which one forms apt beliefs, doubts, and reactive responses and one's *motivationally organizing* desires, concerns and affections.
- Wrongs of "silencing":
  - the successfully gaslit person will not be able to engage, for instance, in acts of "telling" or "protesting," as nothing she does will count as such
  - existential silencing: someone who is gaslit will not be able to take her own thoughts and reactions for what they are—for instance, she'll be unable to treat her anger *as anger* rather than a mere mental storm
- Grave psychological harm, paradigmatically severe clinical depression.

A single instance of gaslighting may not involve every one of these wrongs. For instance, because gaslighting doesn't always involve the use of oppressive social norms as tools, it doesn't always involve the political wrongdoings that are implicated when it does. Structurally speaking, however, gaslighting is no different in this respect from many other interpersonal phenomena. Being angry with someone doesn't always involve the experience of wanting to demand an apology or "feeling steamed," but we'd still think an account of anger that didn't mention these elements had failed to capture something important about what it is to be angry. We have no reason to expect the immorality of gaslighting to be less complex than its interpersonal features or less complex than the interpersonal features of an everyday attitude like anger.

That said, every case of gaslighting will involve some particular version of nearly every wrong on the summary list. Even if, for instance, a given case of gaslighting doesn't involve manipulative appeals to the target's empathy, it will—as we saw in chapter 4—involve the gaslighter making manipulative use of other dispositions that are central to the target's abilities as deliberator, moral agent, and valuing agent more generally. In fact, there are only three kinds of wrongdoing on our list that are not implicated in every case of gaslighting. The first are the specifically political ways in which gaslighters wrong their targets (and others) when they make use of oppressive social norms or stereotypes as weapons in gaslighting. The second is the wrong of deception. While most cases of gaslighting involve outright deception or deceptive pretense, it may be possible to gaslight without employing either of those tools. Third, while successful gaslighting causes serious psychological harms (paradigmatically, clinical depression) and always involves *aiming* at the grave psychological harm involved in radically undermining someone as deliberator and moral agent, unsuccessful attempts at gaslighting do not always result in psychological damage of the former sort.[41]

What shall we say about the relationship among the remaining, quite long, list of wrongs that are always involved in gaslighting? A certain reductionist spirit might lead one to want to claim either that there's some sense in which one of the wrongs on the list is the "core" wrong and the rest are merely knock-on effects or that other items on the list are just further specifications of particular dimensions of that "core" wrong. In fact, however, neither of these tactics offers a promising way of keeping the phenomenon in view. The claim that all but one of these wrongs are mere knock-on effects can't get off the ground. It's true that some of these wrongs stand in a relationship to one another such that wherever there is the one wrong there's the other. For instance, you can't make someone complicit in their own undoing without also violating their rights of self-determination—the former wrong always entails the latter. Similarly, the particular *way* in which the gaslighter induces his target to collude against herself always involves the moral perversity of using deliberatively, evaluatively, and motivationally basic dispositions (like love)

41. Unsuccessful gaslighting will also not involve the silencing of the target in Langton's sense or the existential sense discussed. But since *aiming* at silencing of this sort is inextricable from the gaslighter's characteristic aim of undermining the target as deliberator and moral agent, gaslighting will always involve the wrong of *aiming* at the silencing of the target.

in ways that undermine the agent's abilities with regard to those dispositions (e.g., her ability to love well).[42] But such reciprocal relationships among subsets of the wrongs on this list can't be made to extend to the whole (and then there's the question of on what basis we'd determine which of the wrongs that do reciprocally implicate one another is somehow more central in gaslighting). For instance, being made to collude against oneself in the manner and by the means employed by gaslighters—through appeal to the target's basic evaluative and motivational dispositions—doesn't necessitate also being wronged by being framed as "crazy" (in the sense of a proper object of treatment and management) in the way the gaslighter does, much less being induced to so see oneself.

What about the strategy of trying to identify one "core" wrong on this list and treating the rest as mere further specifications of that wrong? Suppose we said that it's the fact that gaslighting violates the target's right to self-govern that's the core wrong. There are an enormous number of ways of doing that that are nowhere near the territory of gaslighting or the kinds of wrongs it involves, even when it comes to questions of self-government. Tripping me so I can't get where I'm going violates my rights to self-government. Suppose we then add that gaslighting is the kind of violation of one's rights of self-government that involves undermining my ability to self-govern. Still, we're nowhere near the distinctive wrongs of gaslighting. After all, shooting someone in the head also interferes with their

42. That multiple wrongs can be coextensional in this fashion is not unique to gaslighting. Spousal or child abuse, for instance, is always both wrong in its physical/psychological harms and an act of betrayal.

ability to self-govern. We *could* continue on in this fashion, trying to get the whole phenomenon in view with further specifications that it is the *kind* of violation of one's ability to self-govern that's at issue in gaslighting. So, one might say, it's the kind of violation not only that aims to undermine one's ability to self-govern but more specifically a violation that aims to do so in such a way that focuses especially on one's deliberative abilities and moral agency, that does so by framing one as an object of treatment and management rather than a moral agent, that does so by trying to make the target view herself in those terms and by making her collude against herself, and so on. One could, in other words, try to make it out that the "core" wrong at issue here is a violation of a person's rights of self-government, but that it's the *kind* of violation of one's rights of self-government that one can only get properly into view by specifying that it's the *kind* of violation of one's rights of self-government that also involves all the other wrongs on our long list. This move strikes me as obfuscating rather than clarifying. First, many of the other wrongs of gaslighting on our list—wrongs that the imagined interlocutor proposes to treat as specifications of the kind of violation of rights of self-government that's at issue in gaslighting—can't plausibly be understood as such without loss of moral meaning. To say, for instance, that what's wrong with the way the gaslighter weaponizes dispositions that are fundamental to his target's abilities as a deliberator, a moral agent, and a valuing agent more generally in order to undo her as deliberator and moral agent is just that this is a specific way in which her rights of self-government are violated is to occlude the deep kind of moral perversity that we've seen is at issue in this aspect of gaslighting.[43] Moreover, if the claim is that the immorality of gaslighting consists in its being a particular kind of violation of one's rights of self-government, where the "kind" in question is specified by the aggregative total of all the wrongs discussed in this chapter, it's not clear what's to be gained by calling that aggregative total a particular kind of violation of one's rights of self-government. Such a theoretical superstructure might be illuminating for some theoretical purpose, but it's not morally illuminating.

The moral truth about gaslighting is ineliminably complicated. It is a multidimensional horror show.

43. I am reminded of a parallel from Christine Korsgaard's lectures on Kant's ethics many years ago. On a certain reading of Kant, she pointed out that what's wrong with proposing to oneself "I shall kill the person ahead of me in line for the job in order to get the job" is that it amounts to a kind of free-riding—the intention can bear its intended fruit only on condition that others (especially those in line behind one) don't form the same intention. However true that may be, she rightly pointed out, surely *that* is not what's wrong with killing the person ahead of you in line for a job. And so here too: it may well be a violation of my rights of self-government to use my commitment to the deliberative principle that I might be wrong to undermine me as deliberator or to use my love to undermine my ability to love well, but that hardly seems to adequately capture what's wrong with doing such things.

7

Trust and Gaslighting, Revisited

I know I am working with a client experiencing long-term gaslighting when they say things in therapy such as: "I know I have no right to feel this way, but when I show you this text he sent me, it will make more sense."

—DURVASULA, 2021

THE DAMAGE that gaslighting wreaks often shows up most vividly, as it does in the exchange above, in a therapeutic context. We could characterize the psychological injuries on display here in various ways. For instance, we might note what's right on the surface: the gaslit client doesn't feel entitled to her feelings. But we could also talk about this exchange in terms of what it reveals about the damage that being gaslit has wrought in terms of the client's ability to trust. It's tempting on that score to say something like "she was gaslit and now she can't trust anyone, including herself." And yet notice that that would actually be an inapt description of the client quoted.

Sure, in some sense she doesn't trust her own response to the words of the man behind the text ("I know I have no right to feel this way"), but she also thinks her response makes sense ("when I show you his text, it will make more sense"). She doesn't trust her therapist to "take her at her word," instead feeling the need to produce evidence, but she's in therapy and in that sense reaching out *in trust* to a therapist. In fact, in one respect she seems to trust her therapist *more* than herself—the gesture above conveys the sense that the gaslit client needs confirmation from the therapist in order to trust her own reaction. Even at its most successful, gaslighting doesn't eliminate its target's ability to trust: it makes a devastated mess of it.

That's not terribly surprising for a variety of reasons, including the fact that trust seems to play a peculiarly important role in gaslighting. This chapter is devoted to a close examination of just what it is about both trust and gaslighting that makes it the case that trust plays such a significant role in gaslighting, as well as an examination of the nature of that role and a close look at the characteristics of the devastation gaslighting wreaks on its target's trust.

To make progress on these fronts, I'll argue that we need to focus our attention on three features of interpersonal trust that have not been previously noticed. I call these trust's normative framing feature, it's shape sensitivity, and its demand for particularity. Very roughly, we can characterize these features as follows. Trust's normative framing feature has to do with the fact that under the right relational conditions, trusting someone makes it possible for them to wrong you in ways that would not qualify as wrongdoings if you didn't trust them. Trust's shape sensitivity has to do with the ways in which our trust in someone, in scope and content, is responsive to evidence not just about whether they are trustworthy but also with what they can be trusted. For example, we don't simply stop trusting the friend who is chronically late, though we do stop trusting her to be on time. Finally, trust's demand for particularity has to do with the fact that it's a condition on the intelligibility of trust that one be able to specify something in particular with respect to which one trusts a person. If, for instance, you tell me that you trust someone as a colleague but deny that you trust her with respect to any particular matter that being a colleague involves (like adhering to policy or doing her work), I'm not going to be able to make sense of your claim that you trust her as a colleague.

Gaslighters exploit these three specific aspects of trust, and they do so in ways that leave the target neither quite trusting nor distrusting their gaslighter. Instead, the gaslit find themselves tossed between trust and distrust, unstably occupying a world between the two and desperate to find some fixed point on which to focus and ground *either* their trust or their mistrust. This is especially true in cases where there's a close personal relationship between gaslighter and target, but it is also an aspect of the dynamics in less intimate contexts like the workplace which rely on mutual trust to function well.

My entry point to discussion of these issues in section 1 is reflection on two features of trust. The first is the fact that trust is more than reliance or prediction—in some sense, trust has a normative edge, such that violations of trust are appropriately met with anger, disappointment, feelings of betrayal, and the like. Puzzles begin to arise, however, when we try to go beyond this most generic and general description of trust's normative import. The second is the fact that the scope of our focus varies. In some cases we trust a person with this or that (say, with my plants), in other cases we trust someone in a role (say, "as a colleague" or "as a friend"). Both of these familiar features of trust, we'll later see, play important roles in gaslighting. But these familiar features of our everyday practices around trust also naturally raise questions to which there aren't obvious answers. In section 2, I argue that we can answer those questions if we think about trust as a normative framing attitude. With these insights about trust in hand, I turn back to gaslighting. In section 3, I argue that gaslighters often exploit the normative framing dimension of trust and do so in ways that implicate particular aspects of the two familiar features of trust with which we began our discussion. In section 4, I consider several scenes from the movie *Gaslight*, arguing that in each there's a moment in which Paula is both self-assured and experiencing one or more negative reactive attitudes— e.g., anger, resentment, indignation, rage, and/or moralized hurt feelings. This raises a question: why, in these particular moments—in the midst of being gaslit—is Paula able to summon up these emotions of blame and sense of self-assurance, whereas she's otherwise just falling apart? Section 5 answers that question by drawing attention to the ways in which trust's shape sensitivity and demand for particularity are playing a role in these scenes. In short, Paula is able to be self-possessed and call up appropriate reactive attitudes in these moments because these are a few fleeting moments amid otherwise total chaos in which she is able to give some shape and particularity to her trust. In section 6, I draw a few final lessons about gaslighting.

1. Two Familiar Features of Trust and the Puzzles They Raise

A. *Trust's Normative Import*

In this section, I want to highlight two familiar features of trust and show that each raises a question to which there is not an obvious answer. The first feature is just this: trust has normative import. That is, trust involves more than relying on someone in the way we rely on the lights to come on when we flip the switch. Trusting involves having normative expectations *of* someone, such that if they violate one's trust, one will experience some negative reactive attitude in response—anger, resentment, feelings of betrayal, disappointment, hurt feelings, or feeling let down. Sometimes the normative expectations are justified; sometimes they are not.[1]

At the same time, the *kinds* of normative expectations that are involved in trusting someone range widely. To see in what sense this is true, and what's puzzling about trust in this regard, let's start with a simple contrast case: making a promise. Under normal conditions, a promise generates an obligation and accordingly a particular kind of normative expectation; those to whom a promise is made can appropriately *require* or *demand* something of you (that which has been promised). People who break promises are thus rightly subject to resentment, indignation, anger—reactive attitudes that are paradigmatically keyed to the violation of obligations.

---

1. This point was most famously made in Baier, 1986.

Matters aren't so simple when it comes to trust. Consider the differences among the normative expectations at issue in the following examples. Suppose I'm making plans with a friend. I trust they will make proposals for joint activities that take into account my preferences, just as I try to take into account their preferences. If I discover that my friend was proposing activities without any consideration of my preferences, I might feel hurt. Depending on the details of the story, my hurt feelings might be reasonable—after all, if you cannot trust a friend to take your preferences into consideration at least some of the time, they're not your friend. Perhaps the person with hurt feelings is respond-ing to the sense that their friend rarely takes their preferences into consideration. But feeling angry or betrayed in response to a single such instance? That doesn't seem appropriate because although friends are obligated to take one another's preferences into consideration some of the time, it's not obvious they're obligated to do so in every particular instance—there are other ways of negotiating joint activities.

Suppose instead it's a department jointly deciding who will teach what next year. Here too I might trust my colleagues to consider something beyond their own preferences, namely the department's needs, in making proposals for what they will teach. And here too it's not clear they're obligated to do so in this particular instance—if they never consider the department's needs, they're a bad colleague, but they're not obligated to do so every time they act as a department member. Yet it would be odd if I reacted to the discovery that a colleague didn't con-sider the department's needs in making proposals about their teaching with hurt feelings. The register of "hurt feelings" be-longs to a more personal relationship than that of colleagues. The normative expectation at issue here is such that its violation is more properly met with something like feeling put-off or annoyed.

Here's another example. There's a scene in the sitcom *New Girl* where the lead character Jess learns that her best friend saw a long-anticipated movie with someone else before her and is quite hurt. No explicit agreement had been made. But the audience, Jess, and indeed her friend (who "confesses" this amid a fight about other things as a way of lashing out) all see Jess as reasonable in trusting that they would see the movie for the first time together. It's just "that kind of friendship." And so we see Jess's hurt feelings as reasonable, though it would be odd to think that Jess could have appropriately *demanded* her friend see the movie with her first.

On the other hand, sometimes the normative edge of trust is like that of a promise, in being appropriately characterizable in terms of one person's having an obligation (the trusted person) and another's being positioned so as to appropriately demand that the first meet their obligation. Imagine discovering that a friend has been maliciously gossiping about you.[2] Friends are obligated not to do that, and part of what that obligation involves is being appropriately attuned to the fact that we are *trusted* not to do such things. That's why discovering a friend has done such a thing results in not only anger but also *feelings of betrayal*. Feelings of betrayal are the characteristic response to fractures in trust that involve the violation of an obligation.[3]

---

2. This is one of Scanlon's (2008, Kindle locations 1327–1332) most famous examples.

3. However, feelings of betrayal aren't always appropriate, even when obligations have been violated. I trust my friends to show up on time when we make plans. They're obligated to do so. But "feeling betrayed" by a friend showing up late without excuse for a casual coffee just once would be overwrought.

Now, one might think that the problem here—that which is making trust seem puzzlingly complicated in its normative import—is just the fact that promising is the wrong kind of comparison case to illuminate the normative import of trust. After all, promising differs from trusting in ways that might lead one to expect differences in their normative import. For instance, nothing in particular needs to be true of the relationship between promisor and promisee in order for a promise to generate an obligation: a promise made to my enemy or a stranger obligates, just as does a promise to a loved one (and that's true even if there are role obligations that make breaking a promise to a loved one especially serious). Not so with trusting—the relationship between trusted and trustor matters a great deal to whether the normative expectations involved in trust are justified. Suppose, for instance, that I'm negotiating to buy something from a neighbor whom I take, without good reason, to be a friend. That presumption of friendship will lead me to trust them in ways I wouldn't trust a stranger and so feel hurt on discovering they made an exorbitant profit on the deal. But my hurt feelings wouldn't be justified because it's inappropriate to trust acquaintances in negotiations the way we trust friends. In other words, there are background relational conditions that have to be in place for trust's normative edge to be justified (what are those background relational conditions is a complicated matter, one that depends in part on *with* what we trust someone). Here's a second difference between trusting and promising. *My* act of promising creates an obligation *for me* and corresponding normative expectations *of me*, whereas in trust (when the relational conditions are right) *my* act of trusting creates moral claims *on you* and normative expectations *of you*.

Yet shifting to a comparison case that's closer to trusting in both of those respects won't help us clarify why the normative import of trust is so multifaceted and case-dependent. Take the following example. When my dissertation students give me chapter drafts to read, that act creates an obligation for me and corresponding normative expectations on their part such that if I don't read the chapter they'll be appropriately angry, resentful, and so on. The directionality of this example parallels that of trust, and like trust this is a case in which the normative claims at issue are justified only if certain background conditions are met (I'm not obligated to read the work of just anyone who sends their writing to me). But in this case too, like that of promising, the normative import of the act is simple and clear. In both the dissertation chapter case and that of promising, the act creates an obligation, the violation of which is aptly answered with anger and resentment. Some cases of trust, as we've seen, are like that. But other cases—like that of friends making plans or Jess and her best friend—are not. In those latter cases, it would be inapt to speak in terms of obligations violated, the normative expectation at issue in those cases isn't characterizable as something properly demanded of another, and the violation of that normative expectation isn't such as to make appropriate feelings of anger, resentment or betrayal.

So, what sort of attitude is trust, such that acts of trusting give rise to this wide variety of different kinds of normative expectations in seemingly case-dependent ways?[4] We'll return

4. Other attempts to take on something like this question strike me as missing the mark. Darwall argues that we should see trust as a "second personal attitude of the heart"—one that involves having hopes of someone, but which cannot obligate. He tries to make sense of the fact that violations of trust are sometimes met with anger or resentment (paradigmatic responses to the violation of obligation) by

to this question in section 2, but first we need to get another feature of trust on the table.

B. The Focus of Our Trust

Here's a second familiar feature of trust: the focus or scope of our trust is more variable than that of other attitudes. Some attitudes are characteristically person-focused. We love or hate people, for instance. Some attitudes are characteristically action-focused. We are angry at persons, but the focus of our anger is paradigmatically something in particular they did. In contrast, the focus of our trust seems to be more or less action-

---

pointing out that role obligations are often *also* in play when one's trust is violated. The thought is that when I'm angry about someone's violating my trust, what I'm actually angry about is the fact that there is some other feature of the situation that "triggers some obligation of relationship." For instance, in the case of the maliciously gossiping friend, we trust friends not to do that, but independently of our trusting them, they're obligated not to do that. On Darwall's view, anger in this case is appropriately keyed not to the violation of trust but to the independently grounded obligation not to viciously gossip about your friends (Darwall, 2017). But I think this way of dividing up the normative territory won't work. First, the sine qua non of responses to violations of trust is feelings of betrayal, and feelings of betrayal are paradigmatically responses to violations of obligation. Second, most intimate relationships are partly normatively defined *by* trust. If I feel betrayed on discovering my friend viciously gossiping about me, am I warranted in feeling that way because I trusted him or because "some other element triggers some obligation of relationship"? The question doesn't make sense—without trust of precisely this sort, there wouldn't *be* a relationship in which one has obligations of the kind that have been violated. Thus it is that in the face of such violations one says, "I thought you were my friend."

Richard Holton's analysis of trust suggests the possibility of a different strategy. He contends that we should think of trust as "involving something like the [Strawsonian] participant stance." Later he suggests that trust is "part of the participant stance, in the sense that trusting someone is one way of treating them as a person" focused in some cases, and more or less role-focused in other cases.[5] We may, for instance, trust someone as a friend or as a gardener. Or we may trust someone "with" a task or activity— say, watering our plants or the company's finances. Of course we might *say* "sure, I trust her" in response to a query. But in so answering we don't mean that we trust that person with respect to *everything*—that's idealization or hagiography, not trust. Rather, it's the fuller context that settles that with respect to which we trust someone when we make such remarks. If you ask me if I trust a professional colleague and I say "sure, I trust him," I'm conveying that I trust him as a colleague, with no implications one way or the other as to whether I think he's, say, a trustworthy parent. Sometimes, we hedge in ways that clarify the focus of our trust. If you ask me whether I trust a colleague and I respond, "With what?," one reasonable interpretation is that I don't generally trust her as a colleague,

---

(1994, 66, emphasis added). The basic idea here is that (unlike mere reliance) trusting someone is one way of interacting with them as a responsible agent—an individual properly subject to blame. Something like this seems right to me. But it's more a way of pointing to the phenomenon we're trying to illuminate than an illumination of that phenomenon.

5. In the literature on trust, these differences are often captured by talk of trust as a three-part relation, viz., "I trust so and so with thus and such," vs. trust as a two-part relation, "I trust so and so," or two-part relation but in a role, viz., "I trust so and so as [e.g., plumber]." There's an ongoing debate on this score: one side arguing that all cases of trust are, in spite of appearances, two-part relations, the other side arguing that all cases of trust are, in spite of appearances, three-part relations. I find both sides of that debate implausible, for reasons suggested above. Instead, I think once we see that trust is a normative framing attitude, we'll see that it is, *for that reason*, sometimes a two-part relation and sometimes a three-part relation. See, e.g., Baier, 1986; Holton, 1994; Jones, 1996; Domenicucci and Holton, 2017.

though perhaps I do trust her with some particular professional task.

At first glance, then, it looks like we trust people either in certain roles or with respect to specific tasks/activities. But in at least three respects, matters are often more complicated than this. First, when it comes to trust in a role we routinely allow for exceptions within the rubric of a given role. For instance, "Do you trust your plumber?" "Well, sure, except when it comes to the garbage disposal—she's great about everything else." Or, "He's a really trustworthy friend, except when his relatives get involved."[6] Second, we often come to trust people whom we first trust in certain roles in ways that have nothing to do with those roles, as when we learn to trust a colleague's judgment about, say, restaurant quality. Third, social conventions about the expectations affiliated with particular roles are typically mere starting points for parties to a trusting relationship. Parties to the relationship can, for instance, reject some of those social conventions as a matter of mutual understanding. Straight married people, for instance, can reject the sexist convention that she's to be trusted with household chores and he with the finances.[7] But social conventions also provide only the starting point in trusting relationships—especially intimate ones—in the sense that with what intimates trust one another typically goes far beyond what might be specified by reference to social conventions. Some of the most important aspects of any given

6. The latter example is drawn from Domenicucci and Holton, 2017, 156.

7. There are limits here. Parties to a relationship who reject too many of what in their social milieu are regarded as core expectations of that relationship type will have difficulty making themselves intelligible to others. Unconventional marriages, for instance, run into this problem.

friendship are built up slowly out of peculiar-to-those-friends patterns of activities and shared understandings that give rise not only to reasonable (normative) expectations over time but to the particular kind of reliance and "counting on" that's involved in trust.[8] I have friends I trust to comment on my philosophical work, to look after my cats, as political coconspirators, as travel partners, to be a sympathetic ear, to be the personal equivalent of a "wartime consigliere," for late-night phone conversations, for mutual kvetch sessions, or for baking fests. None of these are part of a culturally shared understanding of ways in which friends, as such, trust one another. Friendships can and do thrive without any of these particular normative expectations. But each of the items I just listed gives content and texture to those friendships: they are important to making those different friendships what they are.

So, what is it about trust that makes its focus recognizably flexible in these ways?

2. Trust as a Normative Framing Attitude

The answer to both questions from section 1 lies in the fact that trust is a normative framing attitude. I introduced this feature of trust early on by remarking that it involves the fact

8. Scanlon offers similar examples involving the ways in which participation in joint activities can establish normative expectations that allow one to appropriately count on another. Scanlon is making a point about the ways in which something with the normative force of a promise can be generated without explicit agreement or the speech act "I promise." My point above about the ways in which the activities of friendship can appropriately give rise to normative expectations in the "trusting" territory doesn't presuppose that the normative *force* of those expectations will be the same as that which is at issue in promising (Scanlon, 1998, 297ff.).

that under the right relational conditions trusting someone makes it possible for them to wrong you in ways that would not qualify as blameworthy if you didn't trust them. Let me elucidate. We respond with blame or praise, anger or gratitude, love or hatred, resentment, indignation, hurt feelings, disappointment, guilt or contempt (one of the reactive attitudes) when we take it that someone's conduct or attitudes or character in some way expresses good or ill will (to borrow Strawson's phrase). The forms of good or ill will that someone's conduct, attitudes, or character can express are as various as the reactive attitudes with which we respond to them—from neglect to malice on the negative side, from ordinary due care to heroic acts of bravery and kindness on the positive side. To say that trust is a normative framing attitude is to say that trust changes *what counts* as good or ill will and/or in what *way* someone's attitude or conduct so qualifies. Or, we might say, what trust does is make certain kinds of conduct or attitudes morally salient where that conduct either wouldn't otherwise be morally salient or else wouldn't be salient in the same way. In the best case—the case where the trusting party is clearly *justified* in treating something as morally salient on account of her trust—this will reflect a shared understanding about the normative framework that their trust places on the relationship.

Here, for instance, is a case in which trust makes conduct morally salient that wouldn't be in the absence of trust. I talk with my sister at least once a week, and though we have no explicit agreement, I know that she trusts me to do my part to make sure that happens. If I completely dropped the ball, she'd reasonably feel hurt and disappointed. Her trusting me with this is relationally appropriate, I know she so trusts me, and together those considerations make my calling or not something that can qualify as an expression of good or ill will in Strawson's sense. In this case, the trust goes both ways, and so if she dropped the ball, I'd feel hurt and disappointed. Take trust completely out of this relational equation and "calling weekly" may have no moral salience whatsoever—no more taken by either party as an expression of good or ill will than would be the color of the envelope on a birthday card.[9]

In other cases, trust makes someone's conduct salient *in a way* it would not be but for trust. For instance, I can properly normatively expect of anyone that they won't engage in picture-hiding ruses with me, but it's only insofar as our relationship is a personal, trusting relationship that I can appropriately feel *betrayed* by their doing so. Here, trust changes the normative situation by *broadening* the range of reactive attitudes that can be situationally appropriate.

In these respects, trust transforms the normative landscape between trusted and trustor: hence the phrase "normative framing attitude."[10] Recognizing this important feature of

9. Of course, there are other considerations that could make "calling weekly" morally salient—e.g., an explicit agreement. The point is that trust, like an explicit agreement, can make morally salient activities that would otherwise have no moral salience.

10. As we've seen, there's a background condition that must be in place for trust to genuinely alter the normative situation, namely, the form of trust at issue must be relationally appropriate. One might instead be tempted to say that relationally appropriate trust is a normative framing attitude. I think that would be a mistake. That way of understanding the normative structures around trust misses, or glosses

trust then provides straightforward answers to our questions from section 1. The fact that trust is a normative framing attitude explains why the normative expectations to which it gives rise can vary so greatly. In the good case, there are delicate, and often implicit, interpersonal dynamics that help to settle the various dimensions of the ways in which trust normatively frames their relationship. What gets thereby settled will include both what the parties trust one another *with* as well as the normative import of each activity or item with which they trust one another. For instance, thus and such is the sort of thing we trust one another with in the way that violating that trust makes one appropriately subject to anger; this other thing we trust one another with in the way that its violation licenses (instead of anger) hurt feelings. Similarly, once we see that trust is a normative framing attitude, it's not surprising that sometimes our trust is focused on particular activities, in other cases on the roles in which we stand to one another, and in some cases on a combination of roles and activities. The fact that trust is a normative framing attitude means that any of these might be made, by trust, a matter of good or ill will.

---

over, the fact that relationally *inappropriate* trust will *seem* to the person who trusts to alter the normative situation. If, for instance, my stalker feels "let down" because he trusted me to wink at him in a crowd and I did not, he is entirely without warrant for those feelings. But he *will* predictably feel let down if that's what he, without warrant, trusted me to do. The mere fact that he trusts, albeit inappropriately, is enough to create a situation in which reactive attitudes can come into play where they otherwise would not. In fact, there's a sense in which this means that trust—even relationally inappropriate trust—does alter the normative situation, namely, it alters normative appearances. That fact, as we'll see, is important for understanding some of Gregory's interactions with Paula, and gaslighting interactions more generally.

3. Gaslighting and Trust's Normative Framing Dimension

There are three significant ways in which gaslighters exploit the normative framing dimension of trust. All three are prominently on display in the title movie, and all three are equally recognizable in everyday instances of gaslighting.

First, gaslighters often insist, implicitly or explicitly, that their targets trust them in relationally inappropriate ways and then use that trust—or the target's resistance to trusting in this way—to undermine them. In *Gaslight*, Gregory is a master at this. For instance, in one unnerving series of exchanges, Gregory first tells the maid to send Miss Thwaites—whom Paula has known since childhood and who is trying to visit Paula—away. When Paula twice makes it clear that she wanted to see her, Gregory adduces a string of excuses for sending her away: "I don't think we need to bore ourselves with them," "If you let her in once, you'll always have her here," "I do not want people all over this house!" Then, when Paula protests a *third* time that she wanted to see her, Gregory tells Paula that she should have just said so (pretending she hadn't), adding, "I only thought those people would be a nuisance to you" and that he could call the maid back to "tell her you've changed your mind" if "you're sure you're well enough to see her." There's a lot going on here, including a string of lies and the ongoing attempt to convince everyone (Paula included) that she's unwell. But mixed in with everything else is a bid for a relationally inappropriate form of trust that's easy to miss: Gregory is speaking *for* Paula, without her asking, in spite of her repeated protests, and acting insulted, angry, indignant, and hurt that she doesn't trust him to speak for her about whether she'd like a visitor. The whirlwind of confused excuses combined with the emotional manipulation involved in acting hurt and angry that Paula doesn't trust Gregory to speak for her (in a way he'd have no business doing even if he were the loving husband he pretends to be) are effective. The scene ends with Paula dejectedly muttering, "It doesn't matter."

Gregory's real-life counterparts make similar moves. For instance, in chapter 4 we noted some of the ways in which appeals to authority are used as tools by gaslighters. The scope of a person's proper authority, say in a workplace, can be fuzzy at the borders. One reason for this is that the *roles* that define both the proper bounds of authority and the appropriate bounds for trust in a role can themselves have fuzzy boundaries. Gaslighters use these facts as wedges into relationally inappropriate bids for trust as authority figure, and that trust is then used to undermine the target. Here's one such scenario. A boss who has configured themselves as the employee's mentor first inappropriately pushes the boundaries of that role by insisting that it's better for the employee if they let the boss introduce them to any career connections rather than networking on their own—"just trust me," they say, "it'll be better if we do it this way." The boss then offers to introduce the employee to a particular person at the next company event. No such thing happens at the event, and as the event winds down, the employee gently prods, "Were you going to introduce me to so-and-so?" And the boss retorts blankly, remembering the earlier conversation but acting as though it never occurred, "Why don't you introduce yourself?"

A second way in which gaslighters make use of the normative framing dimension of trust is by acting as though some dimension of their target's relationally appropriate trust in him is *in*appropriate. As we've seen, the particular subject matters of relationally appropriate trust are, to some extent, established not just by general social expectations around relational roles (e.g., friend or spouse) but also by the patterns of activities and habits of the particular partners to a particular relationship. This can sometimes make it unclear whether one's trust is relationally appropriate, even when it is. For instance, what can seem to one friend the sort of thing with regard to which anyone ought to be able to trust their friend (something that's relevantly like "friends don't maliciously gossip behind one another's back") can seem to the other friend like a bid for trust with regard to something that's peculiar to that particular friendship (i.e., relevantly like someone making a bid for the friends to trust one another to comment on their work). People of good faith work through such ambiguities together. People like Gregory, on the other hand, create such situations of unclarity, where matters of trust should not be unclear in this way, and then exploit that situation. Just after the hidden picture scene, for instance, when Paula has been reduced to utter confusion by his producing "evidence" that she hid the painting, she says to him plaintively, "If it's true, you must be gentle with me, please bear with me." If it *were* true that she had hidden the painting, repeatedly, and forgotten about doing so, this would be an entirely appropriate plea of her spouse—a plea to be able to trust in his continued support in spite of her psychological difficulties. What he gives her instead is a look of disdain and an order to go to bed—a cold rejection of her bid to be able to trust him in a respect, and with regard to a matter, that in fact any spouse ought to be able to trust another.

One variant on this theme of the gaslighter exploiting their target's relationally appropriate trust in them has essentially this structure: they make a bid to be trusted in some relationally *appropriate* fashion, fail to act as they were trusted, and when confronted with their failure deny that they made any such bid to be trusted. "Great idea! I'll send it up the food chain," says the boss, who then immediately steals the idea, works it out, and puts it into practice. When later confronted, they respond, "Come on, you should have known how things work around here—if you trusted me, that's all on you."[11]

A third way in which gaslighters exploit the normative framing feature of trust spotlights the trustworthiness of the target of gaslighting. Here the gaslighter first makes a bid to frame certain aspects of their relationship as a matter of his trust in the target and then sets her up to appear untrustworthy *so that* he can act betrayed or hurt. In the title movie, one of the more remarkable examples of this involves a "gift" of a brooch. Gregory gives Paula a brooch claiming it to be his grandmother's (it's not), and Paula is thrilled. He quickly turns to "worrying" she'll lose it, emphasizing how important it is to him. He suggests that she put it in her purse for safe keeping, admonishing her again of its significance. Later, when she's not looking, he takes

11. Notice that this boss's deflection is specifically targeted at the employee's *trust*—the aim is to destabilize the target by creating ongoing confusion about with what, to what extent, and in what roles she can trust the gaslighter. In a different version of the example, the boss's aim would simply be to get the target to believe a lie so that she could get away with stealing the idea. That boss might, like the villain in the movie *Working Girl*, just add another lie, viz., "I hope you didn't misunderstand what you heard. I'm still trying to get your idea through . . . when it's all done, then I'll give you credit!"

the brooch out of her purse and accuses her of not only losing it but betraying his trust that she'd keep it safe. This entire business rests on Gregory's first *creating* a norm of trust between them that she personally keep track of the brooch and placing it in her purse for her to do so.

Gaslighting in everyday life often has this same structure. The boss gives the employee a major project, emphasizing as she does its importance. She then surreptitiously throws as many obstacles in the road of the employee as possible, making it impossible for the employee to succeed. When the employee does fail, the boss says (offhandedly, so as to maximize its effectiveness in undermining the employee), "Huh, I guess we'll have to find something smaller sized to trust you with next time."

4. What the Experience of Recognizing Betrayal Looks Like

Thus far, our reflections have focused on trust and on considering what the moral logic of trust—in particular, the fact that it is a normative framing attitude—can teach us about the ways in which trust is exploited in gaslighting. I want to shift perspectives now and think in the other direction about what gaslighting can help illuminate about trust. And I want to begin in a perhaps surprising way, by taking a closer look at some of the moments in the movie *Gaslight* in which Paula is able to break free of the grip in which being successfully gaslit holds her.

The most notable such scene, of course, is the movie's final scene. Gregory has been caught. Paula and the police know what he was up to—they know that he was trying to drive her crazy in order to have her committed, thereby gaining access to jewels hidden in her attic. The police have tied him to a chair. Paula, in a voice best described as a hiss, says to a policeman, "I want to speak to my husband"—tellingly referring to him by their relationship, rather than his name. She then proceeds to confront Gregory—mercilessly mocking him with a pretense to the madness of which he's accused her and nearly driven her to, taunting him with whether she will set him free, kill him, or turn him over to the police. In the dénouement she yells at him, "Because I am mad I hate you, because I am mad I have betrayed you, and because I am mad I am rejoicing in my heart without a shred of pity without a shred of regret, watching you go with glory in my heart!"

The content of Paula's shouted remarks points us to the nature of the wrong to which she's responding. Her rage-filled mocking pretense to be as insane as he tried to make her, her biting avowal that *she betrayed him*—these are ways of gesturing to the fact that it *is* his fundamental violation of her trust itself to which she's responding. And here Paula is responding not to the violations of trust involved in each of Gregory's specific lies, deceits, or manipulations, but to the way in which he violated her trust precisely by gaslighting her. In gaslighting her, Gregory used the most basic aspects of Paula's trust in him as a weapon against her, for the sake of trying to fundamentally undo her.

There are ways of violating trust that are damaging but relationally survivable: the small-scale lie, the lie that doesn't lead one to think the person has lied more generally, one-off instances of manipulative conduct, and so on. Like a hairline fracture, the injury from a small violation of trust can heal. Then there are ways of violating interpersonal trust that so seriously fracture the relationship that it's impossible to imagine the relationship can continue, and if it does in some way continue it will be as some hollowed-out shadow of what it was or could have been absent the betrayal. Gaslighting is an especially egregious example of a violation of this latter kind, but there are others.

When a violation of trust breaks the relationship in this way, that's nearly always because the relationship itself is partly normatively defined by trust; that is, it is a relationship whose content cannot be specified without reference to reciprocal trust. These are trusting relationships, and what is being employed in cases like these as a tool for ill-treating the other are precisely aspects of that person's trust that play this normatively defining role for the relationship in question. *This* is why when Paula turns to have her final furious conversation with Gregory, she asks for him not by name but by the title "my husband": what's salient at that moment for Paula is her realization that the very aspects of her trust in Gregory through which she has (entirely reasonably) normatively defined their relationship are exactly those aspects of her trust he has used against her.

That angry recognition of the profound level of Gregory's betrayal allows Paula to permanently break free of his gaslighting. But if one watches very closely, there are other, more subtle scenes in which Paula seems to similarly break free of his gaslighting, if only fleetingly. I want to draw your attention to three such moments and show you what I have in mind in part by drawing your attention to the literal expression on Paula's face. By the time any of these scenes occur, Paula is well on her way to falling apart. She floats between bewildered, terrified, confused, depressed, and increasingly childlike interactions with and dependence on Gregory. That's part of what makes each of these three scenes so striking, for in these moments she is suddenly (if all too momentarily) utterly self-possessed. She is also, and I will argue non-coincidentally, unmistakably experiencing flashes of one or more negative reactive attitude: anger, resentment, indignation, disappointment in Gregory, hurt feelings.

In the first our three scenes, Gregory has just accused Paula of having moved and hidden a small painting on the wall and alleges that she's so out of her mind she doesn't remember moving it. Paula manages to assert, "I didn't move it," sternly and with this expression:

The primary emotion expressed here seems to be in the family of hurt feelings, but there's also an element of burning anger in her eyes.

FIGURE 1. "I haven't hidden [the picture]. I swear it. Why should I?" *Gaslight* (1944), directed by George Cukor, released by Metro-Goldwyn-Mayer.

The second scene begins against a background of Gregory having told friends of theirs, including someone very important from Paula's childhood, that Paula is too ill to go to a party, in spite of her having protested otherwise. We see Paula emerge from the bedroom, fully dressed for the party, and determinedly—albeit fearfully—walk into the parlor to tell Gregory she's going. His immediate response is to reiterate that he's already told people she's too ill to go. She says she's going; he says, "Then you will go alone," and to his shock, she responds, "Then I suppose I will go alone." Here's her expression right before she tells Gregory she is going to the party:

FIGURE 2. "I am going to this reception, Gregory." *Gaslight* (1944), directed by George Cukor, released by Metro-Goldwyn-Mayer.

This is a face of great determination and defiance, as well as rage. In a different movie, that facial expression would have been followed by the woman pulling a pistol from her gown. But Paula's tone of voice immediately after flashing that facial expression also adds to this notes of profound disappointment in Gregory as she utters, "Well, then I will go alone."

In the third scene, Gregory comes out directly with the accusation that she's losing her mind and claims that he should have known this would happen because he knows that Paula's mother in fact died in an insane asylum. "That's not true!" Paula yells back. Here is her expression immediately before she does so:

FIGURE 3. "That's not true." *Gaslight* (1944), directed by George Cukor, released by Metro-Goldwyn-Mayer.

Here Paula's facial expression reads as seething wrath verging on hatred and great incredulity, though the watery eyes and downturned mouth also give away her profoundly hurt feelings.

At each of these three moments, however fleetingly, Paula trusts herself, does not trust Gregory, and sees Gregory as having violated her trust. The moments don't last—they are followed quickly by Gregory's making assorted further manipulative gaslighting moves (adducing false evidence, pitting Paula against the servants, pretending he was only kidding, lying, and guilt-tripping) in the face of which Paula's self-assurance dissolves. But I want to focus on those fleeting moments of self-assurance.

5. Particularity and Substance, Shape Sensitivity, and Trust

In the midst of the kind of self-doubt, confusion, radical uncertainty, even increasingly loss of important deliberative skills, and all under the manipulative pressure of Gregory's gaslighting, why is Paula in these moments so utterly self-possessed?

Well, this much is true: in each of these fleeting moments Paula is confident that at least one thing is the case—she did not move that painting, she is well enough to go to this party, and her mother did not die in an insane asylum. Paula is able to be self-possessed in these moments because they are a few fleeting moments amid otherwise total chaos in which she is able to *give some shape and particularity to her trust, to stabilize a situation that for reasons both internal to trust and having to do with Gregory's gaslighting manipulations has had Paula spiraling between trust and distrust.* Let's work our way stepwise up to this thesis.

One interesting feature of trust is that it seems to demand substance or particularity as a condition of its intelligibility. Think about what it's like to interact with someone who says they trust another but cannot tell you anything in particular about which they trust that person. "Sure I trust her," Avi says of Brianna. "But every time she tells you she'll do something she doesn't carry through." "Well, yes, but I trust in her other ways." "She talks maliciously behind your back." "I know, but that's not all there is to her." "Okay, but you know she lies too." "Well, yes, but. . . ." And so on. At a certain point, you literally will not know what Avi means when he claims to trust Brianna. Adding a reference to a relational sphere might or might not help. Suppose Avi tells you he trusts Missy as a professional colleague, but when you ask him about each feature of that role he says he doesn't trust her in any of those respects. So Avi doesn't trust Missy to be truthful with respect to professional matters, or abide by policy or procedure, or act for the sake of organization, or meet her professional obligations if they are disagreeable to her. But, he insists, he trusts Missy as a colleague. If you believe he's being honest, you won't know what he means.

There's a second sense in which trust demands substance or particularity, and that's roughly motivational. When we trust another, trust itself motivates us to seek something substantive and/or particular about which we can trust them. In simple cases—such as my trust in the local barista to sell me caffeinated coffee—the focus or scope of one's trust is so narrow that if one finds one cannot trust the person in some particular, one usually just ceases trusting altogether (finds a new coffee shop). The opposite is true in the case of trusting relationships: in these cases, if we find that we cannot trust someone in one respect, we seek some other particular respect in which we might trust them. "Okay," we think to ourselves, "I can't trust him about that, but. . . ." This tendency is partly explained by the fact that some trusting relationships are intimate relationships like friendships; in those cases, when we find we cannot trust someone in one respect, our love for them will move us to seek alternative ways in which we can trust them.

But this tendency—the drive to find some particular things with regard to which we can trust someone—is also partly a matter of the nature of trust itself. Consider, by analogy, what it's like to find oneself in an angry mood—especially in those moments before one consciously realizes that one is "just in a bad mood." The experience is one of anger looking for an object. Indeed, we sometimes say this to others we recognize are in a "bad mood": "You're just looking for something to be angry about." Trust in the context of trusting relationships can be like that—if there is, in fact, nothing in particular with respect to which we trust the other person, the very fact that we trust them will move us to try to find some such particular respect in which we can trust them.

It shouldn't be surprising that trust has this motivating drive toward particularity. After all, we saw that trust is intelligible only on condition that we can give some answer to this question: With respect to what do you trust her? (whether the answer is in terms of specific activities or tasks, or else a role that implicates substantive normative expectations, like "as a friend"). We are driven to find some particulars in which we can trust someone because this is necessary in order to make our trust of them intelligible to ourselves.

There's one final piece of the trust puzzle we need before we work our way back to Paula and Gregory. Trust is a relation that is shape sensitive: that is, our trust is responsive to considerations that shift its shape and substance.

Let me say a bit more about what this amounts to. We've seen already that there's a demand for particularity that's both an intelligibility condition of trust and an aspect of its motivational upshots. In trusting relationships (that go well) the required particularity can be given (at least in part) by referring to social roles like "friend" or "partner" or "plumber" and their concomitant normative expectations. Domenicucci and Holton rightly note on this score that it would be absurd to think that one could spell out what it means to say "I trust my dear friend" by enumerating all the things I trust him to do, attitudes I trust him to take, and so on.[12]

But let's take a closer look. If I say "I trust my dear friend," you undoubtedly have some idea with what sorts of things, and in what ways, I trust him. And yet, particular friendships are inevitably all somewhat peculiar qua trusting relationships. As I pointed out earlier, the fact that I trust one friend to give me constructive philosophical feedback and count on another to engage in late-night baking fests isn't entailed by what it is to be a dear friend. In a similar vein, if I add to my assertion that I trust her as a friend the caveat "except when it comes to her relatives," your experience of the foibles to which people are susceptible when it comes to their relatives may give you some idea of what I have in mind, in practical and/or affective terms, when I say "except when it comes to her relatives." But unless

12. Domenicucci and Holton, 2017.

I say a good deal more, the exact shape of my trust (or lack thereof) in those respects (when it comes to the "except for(s)") will not be clear. In what ways, exactly, is she not to be trusted as a friend when it comes to her relatives? With regard to what, exactly? Moreover, we are all imperfect, each with our own foibles and flaws, and the shape of our trust will vary from person to person for these reasons as well.

The shape of our trust is appropriately responsive to all of these kinds of considerations, considerations that—on standards that are internal to trust itself—constitute reasons in favor of and against trust. This is easy to see if we think, by way of contrast, about love. If I have a friend who is chronically late, that doesn't give me even prima facie reason to love her less or love her differently. It does, however, give me reason to alter the shape of my trust: even as I might deeply trust her in every other arena and every other respect—I now have good reason not to trust her to be on time. Trust's shape sensitivity can move in the other direction too. For example, I completely trust one of the administrative assistants in my department with every aspect of her job. Recently, we happened to have a brief exchange over something we both saw posted, an exchange that led me in one instant to also trust her completely when it comes to a certain political arena. The relationship has not fundamentally changed. But there is an addition to the shape of my trust—a kind of bubble if you will, added on to the original professional sphere.

These three aspects of trust—its demand for particularity as an intelligibility condition, its motivating demand for particularity, and its shape sensitivity—together make trust especially susceptible to a kind of destabilization that puts the agent not into a state of trust or distrust but rather into an anxiety-ridden, confused, hyperattentive netherworld between trust and distrust.

We can see this by thinking first about what happens when trust is violated. In the face of ordinary violations of trust in the context of a trusting relationship, we can reasonably make one of three moves: forgive, end the relationship, or alter the shape of our trust (as with the friend we trust, except when it comes to his relatives). Even when it is clear that there has been a violation of trust, the appropriateness of choosing one of these options rather than another is often less than clear. And the same motivating forces that drive us to seek out particular respects in which we can trust someone in the context of a trusting relationship—the motivating side of the demand for particularity, our affective or practical investment in the relationship—also tend to move us to *interpret evidence* in ways that are compatible with trusting that person. This, in turn, can make it less than clear that there has been a violation of trust in the first place. In the best case, we call this "giving someone the benefit of the doubt." And of course the motivating force of being in a trusting relationship puts a thumb on the scale of our three options, effectively ranking them in order of preferability from forgiveness first to ending the relationship last. In the context of a decent and healthy enough trusting relationship, that's how it should be.

But not if you're dealing with gaslighters. Not if you're married to Gregory. Gaslighters do everything they can to rationalize the evidence of betrayal, or at least make it seem as ambiguous as possible. They will—as does Gregory—explicitly appeal to the fact of the trusting relationship—"How can you think I would do that?" "You know I love you," or even (in the professional case) "I'm just doing my job" or (in tone of authority) "This is how these things are done"—in order to try to diffuse the appearance of betrayal and remind you of the motives you have for seeking ways in which to trust them. As with nearly everything else gaslighters say, one reason their use of such phrases is so effective in this context is that there are contexts that aren't gaslighting, in which it would be appropriate to say these things. At the same time, the gaslighter will aim at undermining one's self-trust, so that one is increasingly unsure that one is in a position to aptly evaluate whether or not there has been betrayal in the first place.

For the target of gaslighting, the result is a nightmare of utterly destabilized and unfocused trust. Paula's state, in the time leading up to our three key scenes, is just such an unmoored, disarrayed, anxiety-ridden, and confused nightmare. On the one hand, her general attitude toward Gregory continues to be trusting—she continues to see herself, in some nebulous sense, as in a trusting relationship with him. And because she sees herself as in an intimate trusting relationship with him, she is driven to interpret each particular situation accordingly and to continue to look for particular respects in which she can trust him. For instance, in the scene with the missing picture, Paula keeps asking *him* what happened to it. And yet, at the same time, Paula is by this point far too uncertain about the particular facts of the world around her, her relations with others, and her own faculties for her trust to have any definite content. So when she asks him "what happened to the picture?" the tone is in equal parts "I trust you to tell me the truth" and, on the other hand, "can I trust you about this?" There's no anchor here to give content to her trust. That, itself, is radically unmooring, leaving her unsure not only where she stands but also on what basis she could possibly make that determination. This situation is repeated, over and over again. Moreover, as we've seen, Gregory deliberately exacerbates Paula's trust-relevant anxieties not only by playing to her tendency to want to find evidence that exonerates him (a tendency she has precisely because she understands herself as in a trusting, loving relationship with him) but also by manipulating the normative framing features of her trust so as to cause her to be unsure what it is appropriate for her to trust when it comes to him (and so what would qualify as betrayal) and so as to make her seem the untrustworthy one. Her situation thereby becomes one of not only radical uncertainty but uncertainty combined with desperate, anxious attempts to find something in particular about which she may trust him, some way to give some shape and substance, any shape and substance, to her trust.

But then there's this one moment of confidence about *some* fact about the world and herself—*I did not take that picture down*—and in that moment Paula can give one anchor of determinate content to her trust, albeit negative content. "I didn't take it down, and you violate my trust by claiming I did." And so, of course, she is in that moment self-possessed. She is, for that moment, released from the loop of trusting Gregory, but about nothing in particular, seeking to trust him about something in particular, finding evidence of betrayal that he tells her isn't, that the very fact of her trust leads her to interpret as generously (and so ambiguously) as possible, seeking again to trust him about something in particular, finding nothing in particular. . . . For one moment the anxiety-laden question "should I trust?" releases its grip with a firm "here, no."

6. The Inner Workings of Gaslighting, One More Time

There's one final lesson about gaslighting I think can be drawn from all this. Gaslighters chip away at people's sense that they can trust their own judgment. To do so, gaslighters need to destabilize the targets' sense that they know what and whom they can trust. This is both a *means* to undermining the target's deliberative capacities—the very capacities that enable one to occupy a standpoint from which genuine disagreement is possible—and partly *constitutive* of undermining those deliberative capacities. A key step in this process is destabilizing the target's sense of having any determinate content to her trust—anything in particular that she can trust. It's a delicate game, for at the same time that the gaslighter undermines the target in each particular instance, leaving her unsure with regard to that instance whether she can trust the gaslighter or trust herself, he must also continually reinforce the trusting relationship. It is, after all, that trusting relationship that provides the ongoing motivating source for the target's continued efforts to find something in particular with respect to which she can trust him. Insofar as he succeeds, the upshot will be (first) confusion, anxiety, distress, worry, and hyperattention on the part of the target. The gaslighter will then aim to increase the sense of instability in the target's sense of the shape of her own trust, in part by exploiting the hyperattention that's the natural knock-on effect of the fact that her trust has been destabilized. At some point if this continues, the loss of a stable sense of the appropriate shape of her trust (in herself, in others) will itself be a substantial part of the target's loss of practical deliberative abilities. And as a result of all of this, she will be desperate for something, anything, to relieve her distress, her anxiety, her worry, the exhaustion of hyperattention. On this path lie just two possibilities: utter breakdown or total dependence on and enmeshment with the gaslighter.

Particular gaslighters may aim at one or another of these ultimate outcomes—Gregory, for instance, clearly aims at the former, the state that will license him to have Paula committed. Collier, in the movie *Pat and Mike* (first considered in chapter 3), clearly aims instead at total dependence. I want to close by returning to that case.

As a reminder, here's the plot of the movie leading up to the relevant scene. Pat is an expert golfer engaged to a man, Collier, who would rather she abandon her career aspirations, marry him, and devote herself to wifely endeavors. That she doesn't want this for her own life threatens his sense of manhood. So he defensively forms "worries" about her golfing abilities that he frequently expresses to Pat. Pat perseveres and reaches the championship. She's winning. But in the final round, Collier shows up. Right before taking what should have been a final, easy shot, Pat looks up to see Collier's "worried" face. She loses. Afterward, the two have the following exchange on the train:

> COLLIER: How about looking on the bright side of this for instance? Now, take this—as long as your job's out of the way, we move our date up, tie the old knot? I think you've worked long enough, done enough, don't you?
> PAT [distressed]: Oh, too much. [looks down]
> COLLIER [interrupting Pat]: What are you trying to prove, who you trying to lick?

PAT [determinedly, upset]: Myself. [pounds fist
    in air]

COLLIER: You're just the kid who can do it. [puts his leg up,
    his arm around the back of the seat in which she's seated,
    and looks at her both dubiously and patronizingly]

PAT: Collier, do you sort of, I don't think you mean to,
    but do you think of me as just a little woman?

COLLIER: That's right, and myself as a little man. [squeezes
    her shoulders like a small child]

PAT [quite distressed]: Right now I . . . I feel sort of like a
    flop that you're rescuing. I'm flummoxed, that's what
    I am. Maybe we ought to wait until I don't feel so carved
    up, so nobody.

COLLIER: Why don't you just let me take charge!

PAT [fatigued]: I have to be in charge of myself.

COLLIER: Oh what's the good of this? I mean after all, we . . .

PAT: Have to have time to think it over is all.

COLLIER: Well, just see that you don't think it under. It's
    a nice long ride. Just take your time. [opens newspaper
    to end conversation]

This scene nicely illustrates much of what I've been suggesting we can learn about trust from thinking about gaslighting.
Pat, although she's been undermined enough by Collier's
long-standing gaslighting that she loses the key game, nevertheless repeatedly tries to reassert herself. "Myself," she says,
in response to Collier's pointed query "what are you trying to
prove, who you trying to lick?" Pat is trying to find the re-
serves to stand up for herself. She's trying make it true, by saying the person she is trying to beat is "myself," that she can in

fact compete in golf in a way that doesn't have anything to do with Collier. The urgency in her voice speaks in part to her tacit knowledge, spoken through the fog of having been gaslit, that her having just lost the game was (in contrast) about him: it was about, and on account of, his gaslighting. Yet in asserting her aim of making her golfing about "myself," Pat is also thereby telling Collier "on this I shall trust, trust myself" (with literal pounding fist). And in doing that she is also making it clear to Collier that the shape of her trust is *up to her*. As though in direct refutation of that implied assertion Collier responds by literally treating her as a small child—someone who would *need* to *defer* judgment entirely to him. "Just the kid who can do it!," he says, soon thereafter squeezing her shoulders like a small child. The pattern continues. Pat, unsurprisingly, reaches the point of muttering that she feels "carved up," "nobody." This is the point at which, on the model of the way in which trust is exploited in gaslighting that I just sketched, the two future paths further down the road of gaslighting for the target are total breakdown and utter dependence. In a nearly Machiavellian moment, Collier seems to see this and offers the "solution": "Why don't you just let me take charge?"

There's one more relevant parallel in this exchange between Pat and Collier and the scenes between Paula and Gregory. Pat's clearest moments of self-possession in the train scene are precisely those moments where she is responding, in the reactive-attitude sense, to the recognition that Collier has violated her trust. Here, for instance, is the expression on Pat's face in response to Collier's telling her that he does indeed think of her as his "little woman" and squeezing her shoulders like a small child:

FIGURE 4. Pat recognizing Collier's insinuations for what they are. *Pat and Mike* (1952), directed by George Cukor, released by Metro-Goldwyn-Mayer.

Hepburn plays the scene as being back and forth between the disarray of destabilized and shapeless trust and, on the other hand, moments of self-possessed clarity when her trust takes shape precisely insofar as she's able to recognize it as violated. And if the expression on her face here isn't enough to convince you of that, let me tell you how the scene ends. Collier, recall, is making every gaslighting move he can to manipulate Pat into giving up her career and marrying him. After she tells him she needs time to think it over, he responds with a final double-shot manipulative move: insulting her intelligence ("just make sure you don't think it under") and emotionally cutting her off by opening the newspaper with the proclamation "It's a nice long ride. Just take your time." For a moment, Pat sits there stunned, confused, hurt. Then an appalled look suddenly crosses her face. In that moment of realization, she stands up, proclaims, "That's right. And I'm not going to take it!" Then she throws her luggage out the window, and jumps off the train.

FIGURE 5. Pat waves goodbye to the gaslight train.
Pat and Mike (1952), directed by George Cukor,
released by Metro-Goldwyn-Mayer.

7. Regaining Trust after the Gaslight

In the aftermath of gaslighting, it's common for targets to speak of having "lost the ability to trust." That's a quick way of encapsulating what we've seen is a much more complicated truth about this facet of the damage of gaslighting. Trusting well isn't so much a power (like the faculty of sight) as it is a skill—a skill of affective regulation, interpersonal insight, and negotiation, of setting apt normative expectations and revising them where called for, of perception, of moral reflection. In this light, one way of capturing what gaslighting does to trust is to say that it annihilates the skill but leaves the power. It's a power or capacity of a special sort, however. Unlike, say, the capacity to relearn a second language we've lost for lack of use, trust is a capacity we cannot but *try* to act upon. The nature of human life is such that the capacity for trust cannot simply remain fallow, unused. Having lost the skill, but needing as a condition of human existence to exercise their capacity to trust, it should not be surprising that as with other extremely serious psychological traumas, targets of successful gaslighting often present as flailing wildly between utter mistrust and the kind of childlike hagiographic trust that positions another as idealized parent or rescuer.[13] And there is no way around the long road back to the skill. Like a psychological counterpart to physical therapy, it involves relearning how to be sensitive to the fact of trust's normative framing dimension, how to respond in situ to violations of trust in ways appropriately keyed to the attitude's shape sensitivity, and how to fill in the contours of one's

13. Shay, 2014.

trust in another in ways that appropriately meet its demand for particularity. But there is a road back.

In the first instance, the appropriate companions in the difficult work of traversing that road are therapists and friends, not philosophers. And yet clinical psychologists have long understood that when it comes to the process that Freud called "working through," the benefits of being able to name one's experience are incalculable. "Naming one's experience" in this context doesn't just involve literally giving it a name (though that is important)—it refers to the ability to be articulate and specific about the nature of the experience, its effects, and its significance. Moreover, many contemporary clinical psychologists are beginning to understand that the "significance" at issue here—in contexts that involve working through (in the broadest sense)—must include, in one way or another, the social and moral significance of the experience. And in all these respects, the task of "naming" involves the kinds of skills in which philosophers specialize. In that light, it might not be the worst idea to take a little philosophy on the road with you too.

BIBLIOGRAPHY

Abramson, Kate. "Affective Conflict and Virtue: Hume's Answer to Aristotle." In *The Reception of Aristotle's Ethics*, edited by Jon Miller, 222–243. Cambridge: Cambridge University Press, 2012.

———. "Character as a Mode of Evaluation." *Oxford Studies in Normative Ethics* 6 (2016/2017): 56–76.

———. "Correcting Our Sentiments about Hume's Point of View." *Southern Journal of Philosophy* 37, no. 3 (August 1999): 333–361.

———. "Turning Up the Lights on Gaslighting." *Philosophical Perspectives* 28 (2014): 1–30.

Abramson, Kate, and Adam Leite. "Love, Value and Reasons." In *The Oxford Handbook on the Philosophy of Love*, edited by Christopher Grau and Aaron Smuts, chap. 7. Oxford: Oxford University Press, 2018.

Asch, Solomon E. "Studies of Independence and Conformity: A Minority of One Against a Unanimous Majority." *Psychological Monographs: General and Applied* 70 (1956): 1–70.

Baier, Annette. "Trust and Anti-Trust." *Ethics* 96, no. 2 (January 1986): 231–260.

Bailey, Alison. "On Gaslighting and Epistemic Injustice: Editor's Introduction." *Hypatia* 35, no. 4 (2020): 667–673.

Barton, Robert, and J. A. Whitehead. "The Gas-Light Phenomenon." *Lancet* 293, no. 7608 (June 1969): 1258–1260.

Berenstain, Nora. "White Feminist Gaslighting." *Hypatia* 35, no. 4 (2020): 733–758.

Bowles, Nellie. "Thermostats, Locks and Lights: Digital Tolls of Domestic Abuse." *New York Times*, June 24, 2018.

Buss, Sarah. "Valuing Autonomy and Respecting Persons: Manipulation, Seduction, and the Basis of Moral Constraints." *Ethics* 115, no. 2 (January 2005): 195–235.

Calef, Victor, and Edward M. Weinshel. "Some Clinical Consequences of Introjection: Gaslighting." *Psychoanalytic Quarterly* 50, no. 1 (January 1981): 44–66.

Cambridge Dictionary. "Double Bind." 2023. https://dictionary.cambridge.org/us /dictionary/english/double-bind.

Cherry, Myisha. "The Errors and Limitations of Our 'Anger Evaluating' Ways." In *The Moral Psychology of Anger*, edited by Myisha Cherry and Owen Flanagan, 49–65. Lanham, MD: Roman & Littlefield, 2017.

Cooper, Brittany. "Black America's Gaslight Nightmare." *Salon*, September 2, 2015. https://www.salon.com/2015/09/02/black_americas_gaslight_nightmare _the_psychological_warfare_being_waged_against_black_lives_matter.

Crawford-Roberts, Ann, Sonya Shadravan, Jennifer Tsai, Nicolas E. Barcelo, Allie Gips, Michael Mensah, Nichole Roxas, Alina Kung, Anna Darby, Naya Misa, Isabella Morton, and Alice Shen. "George Floyd's Autopsy and the Structural Gaslighting of America." *Scientific American*, June 6, 2020. https://blogs.scientific american.com/voices/george-floyds-autopsy-and-the-structural-gaslighting-of -america/?utm_source=newsletter&utm_medium=email&utm_campaign =today-in-science&utm_content=link&utm_term=2020-06-08_featured-this -week.

Cukor, George, director. *Gaslight* (1944). Released by Metro-Goldwyn-Mayer.

Cukor, George, director. *Pat and Mike* (1952). Released by Metro-Goldwyn-Mayer.

Darwall, Stephen L. *The Second-Person Standpoint: Morality, Respect, and Account- ability*. Cambridge, MA: Harvard University Press, 2009.

———. "Trust as a Second Personal Attitude (of the Heart)." In *The Philosophy of Trust*, edited by Paul Faulkner and Thomas Simpson, 35–50. Oxford: Oxford University Press, 2017.

Davis, Angelique M., and Rose Earnst. "Racial Gaslighting." *Politics, Groups and Identities* 7, no. 4 (November 2017): 761–774.

Dohms, Elizabeth. "Gaslighting Makes Victims Question Reality." *Wisconsin Public Radio*, October 29, 2018. https://www.wpr.org/gaslighting-makes-victims -question-reality.

Domenicucci, Jacopo, and Richard Holton. "Trust as a Two-Place Relation." In *The Philosophy of Trust*, edited by Paul Faulkner and Thomas Simpson, 149–160. Oxford: Oxford University Press, 2017.

Dorpat, Theo L. *Gaslighting, the Double-Whammy, Interrogation and Other Methods of Covert Control in Psychotherapy and Analysis*. Northvale, NJ: Jason Aronson, 1996.

Dowd, Maureen. "Crazy Is as Crazy Does." *New York Times*, May 25, 2019.

Duignan, Brian. "What Is Gaslighting?" *Encyclopedia Britannica*, February 22, 2017. https://www.britannica.com/story/what-is-gaslighting.

Durvasula, Ramani. "Turn Off the Gaslight." *Aeon*, January 15, 2021. https://aeon .co/essays/what-gaslighting-does-in-exploiting-trust-therapy-can-repair

Ferrentino, Danielle. "When America Is Gaslighting You" (October 17, 2018). https://msdanielleferrentino.com/when-america-is-gaslighting-you.

Fine, Cordelia. *Delusions of Gender: How Our Minds, Society, and Neurosexism Create Difference.* New York: Norton, 2010.

Frankfurt, Harry. *On Bullshit.* Princeton, NJ: Princeton University Press, 2005.

———. *The Reasons of Love.* Princeton, NJ: Princeton University Press, 2004.

Frantz, Elaine. "America's Long, Rich History of Pretending Racism Doesn't Exist." *Vox,* May 16, 2019. https://www.vox.com/first-person/2019/5/16/18627753/racism-kkk-police-brutality-sandra-bland.

Fricker, Miranda. *Epistemic Injustice: Power and the Ethics of Knowing.* Oxford: Oxford University Press, 2007.

Gharib, Malaka. "At What Point Does a Fundraising Ad Go Too Far?" *Goats and Soda,* September 30, 2015. https://www.npr.org/sections/goatsandsoda/2015/09/30/439162849/at-what-point-does-a-fundraising-ad-go-too-far.

Girlboss. "How Do You Know You're a Victim of Gaslighting at Work?" *Girlboss,* October 11, 2018. https://girlboss.com/blogs/read/gaslighting-at-work.

Griffith, Megan. "You're Not Imagining It, It's Gaslighting." *Highly Sensitive Refuge,* June 28, 2021. https://highlysensitiverefuge.com/youre-not-imagining-its-gaslighting.

Hammond, Christine. "Gaslighting: How to Drive Someone Crazy." *PsychCentral,* August 12, 2017. https://psychcentral.com/pro/exhausted-woman/2017/08/gaslighting-how-to-drive-someone-crazy#1.

Herman, Barbara. "Murder and Mayhem." In *The Practice of Moral Judgment,* 113–131. Cambridge, MA: Harvard University Press, 1993.

Higgins, Patrick, director. *9 to 5* (1980). IPC Films, distributed by 20th Century Fox.

Hill, Thomas. "Autonomy and Benevolent Lies." *Journal of Value Inquiry* 18 (1984): 251–267.

———. "Humanity as an End in Itself." *Ethics* 91, no. 1 (1980): 84–99.

Hirji, Sukaina. "Oppressive Double Binds." *Ethics* 131 (July 2021): 643–669.

Hochschild, Arlie. *The Managed Heart: Commercialization of Human Feeling.* Berkeley: University of California Press, 1983.

Holton, Richard. "Deciding to Trust, Coming to Believe." *Australasian Journal of Philosophy* 72 (1994): 63–76.

Hume, David. *A Treatise of Human Nature.* Edited by L. A. Selby-Bigge, revised by P. H. Nidditch. Oxford: Clarendon, 1992.

Jones, Karen. "Trust as an Affective Attitude." *Ethics* 107, no. 1 (October 1996): 4–25.

Kelsey-Sugg, Anna, and Areej Nur. "Gaslighting Is 'a Form of Domestic Violence'—and Children Can Be Victims Too." *ABC News,* April 20, 2019. https://www.abc

.net.au/news/2019-04-21/gaslighting-is-domestic-violence-happens-to-children-too-expert/11003116.

Korsgaard, Christine. "The Right to Lie: Kant on Dealing with Evil." *Philosophy and Public Affairs* 15, no. 4 (1986): 325–349.

Langton, Rae. "Speech Acts and Unspeakable Acts." *Philosophy and Public Affairs* 22, no. 4 (1993): 293–330.

Lear, Jonathan. *A Case for Irony*. Cambridge, MA: Harvard University Press, 2011.

Leite, Adam. "Second-Personal Desire." *Journal of the American Philosophical Association* 2, no. 4 (Winter 2016): 597–616.

Litwin, Ann. "The Triple Whammies and Double Binds Faced by Kamala Harris" (November 23, 2020). https://www.annelitwin.com/the-triple-whammies-and-double-binds-faced-by-kamala-harris.

McGlynn, Aidan. "Objects or Others? Epistemic Agency and the Primary Harm of Testimonial Injustice." *Ethical Theory and Moral Practice* 23 (2020): 831–845.

McKinnon, Rachel. "Allies Behaving Badly: Gaslighting as Epistemic Injustice." In *The Routledge Handbook of Epistemic Injustice*, edited by Ian James Kidd, José Medina, and Gaile Pohlhaus Jr., 167–174. London: Routledge, 2017.

McQuillan, Susan. "Gaslighting: What Is It and Why Do People Do It?" *Psycom*, November 2, 2021. https://www.psycom.net/gaslighting-what-is-it.

Mehta, Nicole. "How I Overcame Bullying and Gaslighting in College." *The Perfect Ensemble*, May 22, 2018. http://www.theperfectensemble.net/the-nicole-project/2018/5/22/how-i-overcame-bullying-and-gaslighting-in-college.

Mojtabai, Homa. "Reasons You Were Not Promoted That Are Totally Unrelated to Gender." *McSweeney's*, January 5, 2015. https://www.mcsweeneys.net/articles/reasons-you-were-not-promoted-that-are-totally-unrelated-to-gender.

Moore, Anna. "Abuse Prevention: How to Turn Off the Gaslighters." *Guardian*, March 2, 2019. https://www.theguardian.com/lifeandstyle/2019/mar/02/abuse-prevention-how-to-turn-off-the-gaslighters.

Moran, Richard. *The Exchange of Words: Speech, Testimony, and Intersubjectivity*. Oxford: Oxford University Press, 2018.

Morris, William N., and Robert S. Miller. "The Effects of Consensus-Breaking and Consensus-Preempting Partners on Reduction of Conformity." *Journal of Experimental Social Psychology* 11 (1975): 215–223.

Moye, Kevin. "Racism Denial: A Lesson in Gaslighting." *The Nubian Message*, September 13, 2018. https://www.thenubianmessage.com/2018/09/13/racism-denial-a-lesson-in-gaslighting.

Nall, Rachel. "What Are the Long-Term Effects of Gaslighting?" *Medical News Today*, June 29, 2020. https://www.medicalnewstoday.com/articles/long-term-effects-of-gaslighting.

O'Neill, Onora. "Between Consenting Adults." In *Constructions of Reason: Explorations of Kant's Practical Philosophy*, 105–125. Cambridge: Cambridge University Press, 1990.

Oxford English Dictionary. "Gaslight" (2022 update). https://www.oed.com/viewdictionaryentry/Entry/255554.

Podosky, Paul-Mikhail Catapang. "Gaslighting, First and Second Order." *Hypatia* 36, no. 1 (2021): 207–227.

Scanlon, T. M. "Interpreting Blame." In *Blame: Its Nature and Norms*, edited by D. Justin Coates and Neal A. Tognazzini, 84–99. Oxford: Oxford University Press, 2012.

———. *Moral Dimensions: Permissibility, Meaning, Blame*. Cambridge, MA: Harvard University Press, 2008.

———. *What We Owe to Each Other*. Cambridge, MA: Harvard University Press, 1998.

Shabot, Sara Cohen. "'Amigas, Sisters: We're Being Gaslighted': Obstetric Violence and Epistemic Injustice." In *Childbirth, Vulnerability and Law: Exploring Issues of Violence and Control*, edited by Camilla Pickles and Jonathan Herring, 14–29. London: Routledge, 2019.

Shay, Jonathan. "Moral Injury." *Psychoanalytic Psychology* 31, no. 2 (2014): 182–191.

Simon, George. "A New Form of Gaslighting?" *Counseling Online*, August 31, 2015. https://counsellingresource.com/features/2015/08/31/new-form-gaslighting.

Spear, Andrew D. "Epistemic Dimensions of Gaslighting: Peer-Disagreement, Self-Trust, and Epistemic Injustice." *Inquiry* 66, no. 1 (2023): 68–91.

Stark, Cynthia. "Gaslighting, Misogyny and Psychological Oppression." *Monist* 102 (2019): 221–235.

Steinem, Gloria. "Networking." In *Outrageous Acts and Everyday Rebellions*, 221. New York: Open Road Media, 1995.

Stern, Robin. *The Gaslight Effect: How to Spot and Survive the Hidden Manipulation Others Use to Control Your Life*. New York: Penguin, 2007.

Strawson, P. F. "Freedom and Resentment." In *Freedom and Resentment and Other Essays*, 1–28. London: Routledge, 1974.

Sussman, David. "What's Wrong with Torture?" *Philosophy and Public Affairs* 33, no. 1 (2005): 1–33.

Williams, Bernard. *Moral Luck*. Cambridge: Cambridge University Press, 1981.

Williams, Sophie. "How Racial Gaslighting Invalidates My Experience as a Black Woman." *Cosmopolitan*, October 20, 2020. https://www.cosmopolitan.com/uk/reports/a34368664/racial-gaslighting.

Zeiderman, Lisa. "Gaslighting in the Age of Smart-Home Technology." *Psychology Today*, July 23, 2019. https://www.psychologytoday.com/us/blog/legal-matters/201907/gaslighting-in-the-age-smart-home-technology.

INDEX

9 to 5 (1981 movie), 110–15

abilities, undermined by gaslighting,
10, 12, 14, 19, 24, 30, 36, 38, 43–45, 50,
55, 56, 58, 70, 76–77, 79, 90, 102–3,
106–7, 123–24, 141–42, 145–46,
148–49, 150–51, 154–55, 157–60;
deliberative abilities and, 17, 19, 24,
45–47, 56, 58, 62, 64, 68–69, 76–77,
87–88, 102–3, 106–7, 109, 115, 123,
128–29, 131, 134–36, 138–42, 145,
148–51, 155, 157–60, 195–96; love
and, 157–60; moral agency and,
45–47, 58, 62, 64, 69, 88, 102–3, 106–7,
115, 123, 128, 131, 134–37, 138–42,
145–46, 148, 150–51, 155, 157–60;
self-assurance and, 17, 114; self-
confidence and, 17, 43, 69, 74, 78,
107, 138, 187, 194; self-determination
and, 130, 136, 142, 157, 158–160;
self-discernment and, 136; self-
government and, 129–32, 130, 134,
136, 142, 154, 158–60; trust and, 8,
74, 161–62, 177–78, 195–96, 201–2;
valuing abilities and, 27, 128, 142,
144, 146, 158–60
Abramson, Kate, 1n1, 82n9, 152n39;
Adam Leite and, 145n30

abuse, 22, 27, 29, 158
accountability, 92, 112, 133, 140–41
accusations, issued by gaslighters, 2,
15, 18, 34, 45, 58, 77, 114, 120, 133, 181,
182, 184, 186; accusations of being
unhinged and, 57, 87, 112, 114; accusations of being unwell and, 12, 15,
79, 120–22, 177; accusations of
overreaction and, 1, 18, 34–36, 85,
112, 113–114; accusations of over-
sensitivity and, 35–36, 45, 50, 76,
78, 87, 112, 122, 150; accusations of
paranoia and, 1, 32–33, 35, 45, 76,
78, 80, 83–84, 119–20, 122–25, 127,
131, 133, 135, 150
acknowledgement, failures of in
gaslighting, 41, 46, 48, 70, 107, 113
adaptive preferences, 108–109
affective dispositions, exploited in
gaslighting, 64, 67, 69, 71, 72, 127–28,
148, 155, 192, 201
agency, moral and practical, 45–47, 62,
66, 87, 92, 98, 102–3, 107, 109, 127–28,
134, 136, 139–42, 148–50, 154–58,
159, 191
agent-states, constitutively implicated in the harms of gaslighting,
103, 106

A NOTE ON THE TYPE

This book has been composed in Arno, an Old-style serif typeface in the classic Venetian tradition, designed by Robert Slimbach at Adobe.